HBR Guide for
Women
at Work

Harvard Business Review Guides

Arm yourself with the advice you need to succeed on the job, from the most trusted brand in business. Packed with how-to essentials from leading experts, the HBR Guides provide smart answers to your most pressing work challenges.

The titles include:

HBR Guide to Being More Productive

HBR Guide to Better Business Writing

HBR Guide to Building Your Business Case

HBR Guide to Buying a Small Business

HBR Guide to Coaching Employees

HBR Guide to Data Analytics Basics for Managers

HBR Guide to Delivering Effective Feedback

HBR Guide to Emotional Intelligence

HBR Guide to Finance Basics for Managers

HBR Guide to Getting the Right Work Done

HBR Guide to Leading Teams

HBR Guide to Making Every Meeting Matter

HBR Guide to Managing Stress at Work

HBR Guide to Managing Up and Across

HBR Guide to Negotiating

HBR Guide to Office Politics

HBR Guide to Performance Management

HBR Guide to Persuasive Presentations

HBR Guide to Project Management

HBR Guide for
Women
at Work

HARVARD BUSINESS REVIEW PRESS

Boston, Massachusetts

Copyright 2019 Harvard Business School Publishing Corporation

All rights reserved

Printed in the United States of America

10 9 8 7 6 5 4 3 2 1

No part of this publication may be reproduced, stored in or introduced into a retrieval system, or transmitted, in any form, or by any means (electronic, mechanical, photocopying, recording, or otherwise), without the prior permission of the publisher. Requests for permission should be directed to permissions @hbsp.harvard.edu, or mailed to Permissions, Harvard Business School Publishing, 60 Harvard Way, Boston, Massachusetts 02163.

The web addresses referenced in this book were live and correct at the time of the book's publication but may be subject to change.

Library of Congress Cataloging-in-Publication Data

Title: HBR guide for women at work
Other titles: Harvard business review guides.
Description: Boston, Massachusetts : Harvard Business Review Press, [2019] | Series: Harvard business review guides
Identifiers: LCCN 2018017709 | ISBN 9781633693364 (pbk : alk. paper)
Subjects: LCSH: Women executives. | Women white collar workers. | Career development
Classification: LCC HD6054.3 .H27 2018 | DDC 650.1082—dc23
LC record available at https://lccn.loc.gov/2018017709

ISBN: 9781633693364
eISBN: 9781633693371

The paper used in this publication meets the requirements of the American National Standard for Permanence of Paper for Publications and Documents in Libraries and Archives Z39.48-1992.

What You'll Learn

Unconscious gender biases run rampant in organizations today. Women are less likely to be given credit for their work, tend to command lower salaries, and are less likely to be promoted, especially to key leadership and C-suite positions, than their male colleagues. Because of gender biases inherent in our culture, women often struggle to make their voices heard, avoid getting involved with office politics, and shy away from negotiating for the roles and salaries they deserve. It may feel like there's no way out: When they do speak out or talk about their achievements, women may be considered overly aggressive.

While systemic biases are not women's problem to solve, the reality is that in many cases women must still navigate around them to reach their career goals. If you are a woman and these challenges sound familiar to you, there are ways to develop how you communicate, present yourself, and connect with others so that you can break past these biases and become more effective in the workplace and in more control of your career.

In this book, women will learn to:

- Understand the biases preventing their advancement in the workplace—and the self-defeating behaviors that those biases can trigger

- Come across as more confident by using more definitive, muscular language

- Promote their expertise and experience through a robust personal brand

- Share strong opinions without being perceived as pushy or emotional

- Turn "office housework" requests into real opportunities for growth

- Build a network of support, including relationships with mentors and sponsors

- Display leadership potential through vision and decisiveness

- Strike the right balance between an outwardly imposed "professional" appearance and one that is authentic—especially for women of color

- Work through their hesitation to negotiate

- Respond to an inappropriate, sexist, or racist remark at work

- Encourage their organizations to change

Contents

Contents

SECTION FOUR

Position Yourself for Leadership

Contents

SECTION FIVE

Negotiate for What You Want

SECTION SIX

Navigate Difficult Situations

Contents

Introduction

You sit down in a meeting and begin to speak, describing an innovative new product you'd like to release in the next year. Within a few moments, you're interrupted by a male coworker, and despite your best efforts, you can't get back into the conversation. Five minutes later another male colleague reiterates the need for the new product, and the table nods in acknowledgment, thanking him for his idea.

Frustrated, you walk out of the meeting, feeling more invisible than ever. A moment later, your boss stops at your desk: "The prep work you did for the meeting was really helpful, but next time you present, you should have more confidence. You never got your point across."

Sound familiar? This scenario and others like it are all too common for many women at work, where their ideas aren't heard, feedback is vague, and the road to advancement is long and difficult. Across organizations, women command lower salaries, are less likely to get promoted, and are underrepresented in key leadership positions, including the C-suite.

Some argue that women should lean in or step up, that they lack ambition or confidence. But placing the burden of work to be done on women is unfair and strategically wrong-headed. Most of what holds women back are the unconscious biases against them that are difficult to work around or eliminate. Organizations develop programs and set goals to ensure that women are fairly treated, but time and again, women find themselves facing the same challenges—and watching the men they work with succeed while they are left behind. While much still needs to change with how men, managers, and leaders are responding to and working with their female colleagues and employees, the reality is that these biases exist, and unfair or not, women will be forced to grapple with them for years to come.

But that's not to say women are helpless to these biases—or that they can't improve their situation. This guide aims to help you, as a woman, navigate these obstacles more successfully. It provides the advice and tools you need to more effectively promote your work and ideas, communicate with others, and handle difficult situations that are particular to a woman's experience of the workplace, so that you can be credited for your accomplishments, get more done in your organization, and advance to the level you want. While this book is targeted at women specifically, the final section also includes tips and advice for all leaders and managers—male and female—so they can learn how to change their organizations, work with women more fairly and effectively, and combat the biases that are hindering women's influence and growth.

What's Holding Women Back

Both men and women have been indoctrinated with stereotypical views regarding gender. Historically, men have been breadwinners, while women have been the ones to take care of the family. Over time, these roles have shifted, but the unconscious perceptions behind them have not. In Western society, men are seen as—and trained to be—assertive and in control, often portraying qualities like aggressiveness, ambition, and self-confidence, while women are socialized to be communal team players, where they're expected to be helpful, sympathetic, gentle, and soft-spoken.[1]

Some of this stems from childhood. According to research by professor Deborah Tannen in her classic *Harvard Business Review* article, "The Power of Talk: Who Gets Heard and Why," when boys and girls play, they often group themselves by sex and converse differently. Boys tend to identify a leader and pride themselves in their status; they show off their abilities and tell others what to do. Girls, on the other hand, downplay differences in favor of close friendship. Rarely do you see a girl trying to one-up a peer, for fear that she would draw attention to herself or be considered stuck up or bossy. According to Tannen, girls "learn to talk in ways that balance their needs with those of others—to save face for one another in the broadest sense of the term."

These learned behaviors play out in a number of different ways in the workplace. Women are hesitant to speak up about their accomplishments, presuming that others would recognize their hard work and give them the credit they deserve. They often tweak their language to avoid offending others, for example, by apologizing or presenting requests as questions, rather than commands.

And since those around them expect these communal behaviors of women, they hold their own biases: Women are often not acknowledged for their achievements; rather, their work is considered part of a team effort.[2] They are also assumed to be more likely to step in to help without the benefit of additional pay or promotion, which can lead to exhaustion and burnout.[3] Since women don't speak out in the same way men do, leaders and managers presume women in their organization lack confidence or drive. And when few ask for promotion or advancement, others assume they aren't ambitious or are content with their current level or position in the company.

When women do break free of these social norms and show traditional male leadership attributes, such as self-promotion or strong opinions, they're often punished for it. According to research by psychology professors Alice H. Eagly and Linda L. Carli, they are viewed as "deceitful, pushy, selfish, and abrasive."[4] Women face a double bind: If they're too assertive, they're admonished—but without some level of assertion, they struggle to move up into the roles they want.

These biases play out in much more than acknowledgment of achievements or promotional decisions, though. They see the results of these biases in daily work dynamics as well. Women are held to different standards when it comes to performance. They're interrupted in meetings. They can face inappropriate jokes and sexual harassment. And especially in male-dominated industries, like STEM (Science, Technology, Engineering, and Math), they're skipped over for assignments and skill development, because women are not visible enough.[5]

For decades, organizations have created ways to help women by offering them development opportunities and mentorship programs. And while these efforts should be applauded, they are not enough. It's in everyone's best interest to teach men, managers, and leaders in companies how to get rid of these biases and support women. But this won't happen overnight, and in the meantime, women need ways to navigate these obstacles, so they can set themselves up for the right opportunities and roles.

What This Book Will Do

This book provides practical advice on how you, as a woman, can set yourself up for growth and advancement and surmount the specific barriers holding you back. It helps you break habits and change your behaviors, so you can stand out, align yourself with the right people to ensure career growth, negotiate for the position and pay you want—and build the appropriate communication and leadership skills along the way. You'll also learn how to deal with difficult situations common to women's experiences in the workplace, from handling an unfair performance review to responding to an offensive comment.

While there is no one process to follow to navigate the obstacles holding you back at work, there are key areas on which you can focus your attention. We go through each in turn, starting with how to make sure you're seen by those who matter in your organization and acknowledged for your accomplishments and expertise.

Make yourself visible

Unfair as it is, women often presume that their hard work will speak for itself, while in reality their individual accomplishments are usually glossed over. Self-promotion can seem unpleasant, but there are ways to make yourself more visible inside and outside your organization, without making yourself a braggart.

Section one starts by identifying four behaviors, from being modest to blending in, that may be holding women back from reaching the levels that they want in their career. By understanding how these behaviors are perceived by those around you, you can make slight changes in the way you work that can have a big impact in your career. The next chapter explains how to break free from the habits that were socially pressed on you in school, so you become indispensable to your organization. Last, you'll see how to develop a personal brand and promote it, so you're acknowledged for your expertise and set up for future opportunities—without looking like a craven self-promoter.

Communicate with confidence

Being seen in your organization means little if you aren't also heard. Women are socialized to speak in a way that saves face for others, but those around them perceive this behavior as a lack of confidence and ambition. Section two helps you adjust when and how you speak so you have more influence.

The section begins with an interview with linguistics professor Deborah Tannen about how certain ways women speak may be diminishing their authority. She explains that women may not be less confident, but they're socialized to sound that way. Following that, you'll learn how to overcome many of the communication traps in meetings by making your language more muscular and direct, so you're finally acknowledged for your contributions.

In addition to learning about these linguistic barriers, you'll discover the role emotions play in communication, especially since a woman's passionate tone is often misinterpreted. You'll learn how to share strong views without being seen as emotional and about the importance of warmth in influencing others, for women in particular.

Build a network of support

Moving up in your career isn't something you can do alone, especially as a woman. You need to align yourself with the right people who can help you develop your skills and find the right opportunities for growth. Section three will help you find these individuals and explains how to manage the relationships.

The section begins with a counterintuitive approach to office politics for women. Rather than avoiding politics altogether, build a network that will strengthen your field of influence. It then explains how to select the right set of mentors (yes, you need more than one) by defining what you want to learn and how you plan to work with them. While mentorship will provide you with the right confidants to give you advice, you also need the right sponsor—someone who will open doors and advocate for you. The next chapter tells you how to find this special type of ally.

As you build your network, it's tempting to look for those who are most like you—which may inadvertently mean mostly women. You'll learn why you should target men in your search, since they often have wider ranges of influence. But with such alignments comes risk— especially rumors of sex and personal relationships. The last chapter in this section describes how to offset any potential gossip by telegraphing professionalism.

Position yourself for leadership

Section four helps you learn essential skills, so key stakeholders will see your potential even before you're in a leadership position. But women also bring unique traits to the table that men do not. The first chapter provides a list of these qualities, so you can build on them as strengths.

Women are also often viewed as team players, and while there are arguments for collaborative leadership, leaning solely on the opinions of others can make women appear less decisive than their male counterparts. The next chapter explains how to make decisions without relying on a group's consensus, so you signal your authority to others. You'll also discover tips to help you see the importance of strategic vision and how you can build it.

Of course, certain qualities in leadership are harder to assimilate. Appearance can play a significant role— especially for women of color. The final chapter in this section explains how to balance your own cultural and individual preferences with those of the organization.

Negotiate for what you want

You won't go anywhere in your career if you don't ask—and often these discussions require negotiation, which many women hesitate to do. In research that studied the starting salaries of MBAs who had recently graduated from Carnegie Mellon, men were paid 7.6% higher on average than women. The reason? Most of the women accepted their salary offer with no question; only 7% attempted to negotiate.[6]

Section five provides ways women can better negotiate for what they want, whether it's a new role or higher pay. It starts by explaining why women tend to avoid negotiation and provides a simple language trick to make you more comfortable. Then, you'll discover sample questions you can ask to guide you through the tough conversation of telling your boss what you want. You'll also learn how to negotiate at times when your counterpart may not expect it, particularly when your hard work may not be seen as an opportunity for advancement.

Many women are often asked to help teammates, for no other reason than the assumption that a woman's communal nature would lead them to volunteer their time. The last chapter in this section helps you deal with this "office housework" and describes how to negotiate the request to work in your favor.

Navigate difficult situations

While the advice throughout this book helps you to get the credit you deserve, grab opportunities, and move into the roles you want, many of the challenges women face on a regular basis don't relate directly to career growth and promotion. Section six helps you overcome a number of these issues.

First, you'll learn how to transition back to work after taking time off, particularly when you've been taking care of a child. While women aren't alone in this struggle (men, too, take time off for childrearing), it's common to run into issues securing a job, when HR departments see such a gap on a résumé. This section also teaches you approaches for responding to unfair performance reviews—an often-cited frustration for women at work—and how to prevent them in the future.

You'll also learn how to face uncomfortable or inappropriate behavior in the workplace. The third chapter in this section provides advice on how to respond to an offensive or sexist comment at work, keeping in mind any potential repercussions. You'll read about your legal options if you've been sexually harassed by a boss or coworker. Finally, you'll learn about ageism and how that's holding older women back.

Advice for leaders and managers

The majority of this book is written to help women maneuver around or overcome the difficulties they face at work. But all of us need to work together as a society to eliminate these biases altogether—for men, managers, and organizational leaders to advocate for women, develop them, and get them on the path for growth.

The final section in this book explains how to get these individuals involved. The first chapter discusses how organizations should be educating *everyone* on inclusive behaviors, rather than training minority groups like women to help each other. Next you'll learn how leaders and managers can fight bias without pointing fingers, and get tips on how men can better work with and mentor women. Finally, managers will be able to see where they may be holding women back and how they can offer better opportunities to them in the future.

We'd encourage readers to share these chapters with the leaders, managers, and especially men in their organizations, so they can help make long-term change. By transforming men and others around them into allies, women can gain much more in their career and daily work—and finally break through to the levels of the organization that they deserve.

NOTES

1. Alice H. Eagly and Linda L. Carli, "Women and the Labyrinth of Leadership," *Harvard Business Review*, September 2007 (product #R0709C).

2. Shelley Correll and Caroline Simard, "Research: Vague Feedback Is Holding Women Back," hbr.org, April 29, 2016 (product #H02UUL).

3. Rob Cross, Reb Rebele, and Adam Grant, "Collaborative Overload," *Harvard Business Review*, January–February 2016 (product #R1601E).

4. Alice H. Eagly and Linda L. Carli, "Women and the Labyrinth of Leadership," *Harvard Business Review*, September 2007 (product #R0709C).

5. Shelley Correll and Lori Mackenzie, "To Succeed in Tech, Women Need More Visibility," hbr.org, September 13, 2016 (product #H034AG).

6. Linda Babcock et al., "Nice Girls Don't Ask," *Harvard Business Review*, October 2003 (product #F0310A).

Make Yourself Visible

CHAPTER 1

Why You Aren't Noticed for Your Accomplishments

by Jill Flynn, Kathryn Heath, and Mary Davis Holt

Having combed through more than a thousand 360-degree performance assessments conducted in recent years, we've found, by a wide margin, that the primary criticism men have about their female colleagues is that the women they work with seem to exhibit low self-confidence.

Our gut says that this may partly be a perception issue: We've observed that men sometimes interpret (or misinterpret) an inclination in women to share credit or

---

Adapted from "Four Ways Women Stunt Their Careers Unintentionally" on hbr.org, October 19, 2011

defer judgment as a lack of confidence. Still, perception or not, there is some research to suggest that women themselves feel less self-assured at work than men. An ambition and gender report released in 2011 by Europe's Institute of Leadership and Management revealed that women report having lower confidence in regard to their careers:

- Men were more confident across all age groups, with 70% of males having high or very high levels of self-confidence, compared with 50% of the women surveyed.

- Half of women managers admitted to feelings of self-doubt about their performance and career, but only 31% of men reported the same.

- This lack of confidence extends to a more cautious approach to applying for jobs and promotions. Twenty percent of men said they would apply for a role despite only partially meeting its job description, compared with 14% of women.

Looking back through scores of interviews we've conducted in the course of training and coaching engagements, and returning to the 360 reports, we found four specific behaviors cited by managers (male and female alike) that are giving the perception of low confidence and stunting women's careers.

Being Overly Modest

We see that men are more willing to take public credit for their successes. Women believe their accomplishments should speak for themselves, and they spend less effort ensuring they get the gold star next to their name. While modesty is a nice character trait, it's naive to believe that your boss, your clients, or your colleagues will recognize your accomplishments if you fly under the radar. Take steps to ensure that others see your hard work, and take credit for your achievements.

Not Asking

We've seen it over and over again: Women fail to get promoted because they fail to step up and apply. It feels personally risky to ask for a big job or assignment—but there's really no other way. Not asking means you've lost the chance to influence the outcome.

When Sharon Allen became chairman of Deloitte & Touche USA in 2003, she not only became the highest-ranking woman in the firm's history, she also became the first woman to hold that role at a leading professional services firm. It may seem surprising, then, that even Allen learned this lesson the hard way. As a rising manager in her thirties, she was taken aback when she received a memo announcing the promotion of several close colleagues. She wondered why she didn't make the list. Allen stewed about it for a day or two, and then went in to see her boss.

"I was surprised to see my name not included on the promotion list," Sharon said to him. "I have accomplished A, B, C, D, and E, and I think I deserved that promotion." Her boss replied, "Sharon, I had no idea you had accomplished all of those things. You didn't let me know." When Sharon tells the story today, she laughs and shakes her head. As she told us, "That's the very last time I ever let that happen."

Blending In

Some women go to great lengths to avoid attention. They don't want to stand out—in meetings, in the boardroom, or even in the elevator. A client from one of our workshops told us that her greatest fear was riding the elevator with the CEO. *What would she say to him? Would they talk about the weather?* But blending in means you are missing opportunities—every single day—to stand out and sell your ideas. Another female client we know waits in the lobby many mornings so she *can* ride the elevator with the CEO. Her confidence has never been questioned.

Remaining Silent

It's not easy to get a word in during meetings, especially when six other colleagues are fighting for the floor. But failing to speak up and express yourself when you have something relevant to add is a missed chance to get in the game. Getting your point of view across during important discussions is essential for your career.

What we've found in our work is that career momentum for women is not about adding job skills but about changing everyday thinking and behaviors. The majority of high-performing women don't need to make major changes. Small adjustments in how they think and act can improve not only how confident they seem but how confident they feel.

Jill Flynn is a partner at Flynn Heath Holt Leadership, which specializes in leadership development programs and executive coaching for women. She is a coauthor of *Break Your Own Rules: How to Change the Patterns of Thinking That Block Women's Paths to Power*. **Kathryn Heath** is a partner at Flynn Heath Holt Leadership. She is a coauthor of *The Influence Effect: A New Path to Power for Women*. **Mary Davis Holt, MBA,** is a senior consultant with Flynn Heath Holt Leadership, and she is a coauthor of *Break Your Own Rules: How to Change the Patterns of Thinking That Block Women's Paths to Power*. Follow them on Twitter @FlynnHeathHolt.

CHAPTER 2

Disrupt Yourself— and the Way You Work

by Whitney Johnson and Tara Mohr

Academic institutions are churning out more female graduates than ever. But the very skills that propel women to the top of the class in school are earning them middle-of-the-pack marks in the workplace. Indeed, a Catalyst study found that women account for 63% of middle- and senior-level managers in the United States but only 5.2% of *Fortune* 500 CEOs.[1] Based on our experience, those numbers will continue to improve—but only incrementally—until bias against women is reduced

---

Adapted from "Women Need to Realize Work Isn't School" on hbr.org, January 11, 2013

and women recognize that the boardroom is not the schoolroom. To be successful, we must now do the very thing we were always taught not to: be disruptive.

In business, disruption is a proven path to success: Innovations take root at the low end of the market, or create a new market, and then eventually upend an industry. If you play disruptively as you go into the workplace, you'll be doing the upending.

Consider disrupting yourself when it comes to these five areas—areas where the skills you honed as a high-achieving student are likely doing you a disservice in your career.

Challenge and Influence Authority

In school, in order to get the grade, you learned to provide the authority figure—the teacher—with what he or she wanted. In the workplace, that translates into asking "good girl" questions: What does this boss want from me? Which of my boss's needs aren't being met? What do I need to do to get an A?

This approach may earn you some initial gold stars, but it won't get you what you really want, which is to be an indispensable player—not just to your boss, but in your industry. To become an all-star, you need to develop a new skill: You need to learn how to *challenge and influence* authority, rather than simply give the authority figures what they want.

Once you find problems that need to be solved and think up solutions, it's time to start talking—and especially to start persuading. According to research conducted by Target Training International, the single most important trait serial entrepreneurs possess (and to be successful, the entrepreneurial mindset is required) is the ability to persuade.[2] That means trusting and advocating your ideas, even when those around you hold a different point of view.

Prepare, but Also Learn to Improvise

In school, you prepared as much as possible for the test so you would know the answer to anything you might be asked. In the workplace, not everything you need to know can be found in a textbook. Instead of overpreparing, or dithering out of fear or insecurity, learn to improvise.

We think improv is off the cuff, but any great jazz musician will tell you it is anything but. Improvising takes practice. So try it out when the stakes are lower. Sitting in a meeting and haven't contributed yet? Come up with something to say—and say it right now. Running out of time to perfect that presentation? Don't push back the meeting: plow ahead with what you've got. If there's a cool project you don't quite have all the skills for, volunteer anyway.

For instance, when one young woman in our network was completing an internship in Dubai as part of a graduate program, the company asked her to write a business plan. Her field of study was in international relations, not business. But did she tell them she wasn't qualified? Hardly. She bought a copy of *Business Plans for Dummies* (really) and came up with one. As it turned out, she had quite a knack for business strategy. She enjoyed it so much that she ended up switching fields and getting accepted to a doctoral program at a top business school. She might never have known how much she enjoyed business strategy—or how good she was at it—if she hadn't taken that chance.

Find Effective Forms of Self-Promotion

In school, you learned that if you worked hard and performed well, you got an A on your report card. A's got you into college, and they likely landed you a great job. Performing well was most of what you needed to do. Now, you need to work hard, perform well, *and* make sure people know about your hard work and excellent performance.

Until our culture evolves, as a woman, you'll have to do this within the context of the double bind. You'll often have to do better work than male counterparts to stay ahead, but you'll be shamed or gaslighted if you toot your own horn too explicitly. Find the forms of self-promotion that work—for a woman—within your workplaces. These will likely be subtler than those that typically work for men. For example, you might congratulate your team on their key accomplishments in ways that are highly visible to senior management. Your team members will appreciate the positive spotlight, and at the same time you'll become known as someone who is leading a team to stellar results. Or, showcase your work in ways that are of service to others: Host a lunch for other managers to discuss the useful process your team employs or to present the market insights gleaned in a recent project. Your great work will become more visible but in an organic way that genuinely adds value for others.

Welcome a Less Prescribed Career Path

In school, most students follow a prescribed and universal trajectory: Algebra 1, Algebra 2, Precalculus, Calculus, and so forth. A career path is far less scripted and often full of surprises. Embrace your individual, unusual career path.

When you are scared, consider that to be a good sign. Unlike running with the pack, forging your personal path may feel uncomfortable, but you don't upend anything while clinging to the herd. One of us (Whitney) went from studying music to equity research to co-founding a hedge fund and couldn't be happier now writing, speaking, and advising on innovation. The other (Tara) went from the nonprofit sector to Stanford Business School to launching her own business, training women for leadership and helping them find greater fulfillment in work and life. More and more women are embracing unusual, self-directed career paths that play to their strengths and are aligned with their values.

Aim for Being Respected, Not Just Liked

In school, many of us did what was necessary to survive socially: You may have found yourself swapping being smart for being cool. But in our careers, and over time, we are learning to shoot for being respected by those we work with—rather than striving to be liked by everyone.

To pursue your professional dreams, put what's popular in the back seat. For example, if your gifts and aptitudes lie in areas that aren't seen as "girl appropriate," you may find yourself pulling back. The statistics indicate that many women are doing just that. According to research by the National Center for Women and Information Technology, between 2000 and 2008, there was a 79% *decline* in the number of incoming undergraduate women interested in majoring in computer science, likely because the stereotype of a "coder" is still a geeky white male. Yet nearly any mid-career professional will tell you that knowing how to code opens professional doors, elicits tremendous respect, and ironically, gains you popularity. It's not easy to fight stereotypes, but doing the unexpected is exactly what disruption is all about.

None of this is to say that the skills honed at school are unnecessary. They are vital to both your career and life and were, in fact, the price of entry into the workplace. You have learned to respect authority and rules. You believe effort will be rewarded. You can adapt to others' reactions and opinions. Now it's time to build on those bedrock skills and actively pursue disruption, recognizing that because you are trying something new, you may not make the grade initially. But as you learn to challenge the status quo, think on your feet, forsake popularity, and explore unusual paths, you may just upend your way to a best-in-class career.

———————

Whitney Johnson is an executive coach, speaker, and innovation thinker. She was recently named one of the most influential management thinkers by Thinkers50.

She is the author of *Build an A-Team* and the critically acclaimed *Disrupt Yourself.* Follow her on Twitter @johnsonwhitney. **Tara Mohr** is an expert on women's leadership and the author of *Playing Big: Practical Wisdom for Women Who Want to Speak Up, Create, and Lead,* named a best book of the year by Apple's iBooks. She is the creator of the pioneering Playing Big leadership programs for women, which now have more than 2,000 graduates worldwide. Connect with her at taramohr.com.

NOTES

1. Catalyst, *Pyramid: Women in S&P 500 Companies*, February 2, 2018, http://www.catalyst.org/knowledge/women-sp-500-companies.

2. Bill J. Bonnstetter, "New Research: The Skills That Make an Entrepreneur," hbr.org, December 7, 2012, https://hbr.org/2012/12/new-research-the-skills-that-m.

CHAPTER 3

Develop and Promote Your Personal Brand

by Dorie Clark

As you strive to be both influential and recognized in your company and think about your career trajectory, it's important to ask yourself, What do you want to be known for? How do you want to be seen in your organization? In your field? Your industry? What's your personal brand?

A strong reputation can put you on the radar for exciting career opportunities. When your true talents

---

Adapted from "How Women Can Develop—and Promote—Their Personal Brand" on hbr.org, March 2, 2018 (product #H046PA)

are understood, it's far more likely you'll be tapped for relevant and interesting assignments—and that helps you stand out against a field of competitors. Research by Sylvia Ann Hewlett at the Center for Talent Innovation shows that cultivating your personal brand is one of the best ways to attract a sponsor. And professionals with sponsors are 23% more likely than their peers to be promoted (something we'll discuss more in chapter 10). Your brand is also a powerful hedge against professional misfortune. If there are layoffs or cutbacks at your company, being recognized in your field makes it far more likely that you'll be snapped up and rehired quickly by another firm.

But personal branding has some unique challenges for female professionals. Research has repeatedly shown that women are subject to a phenomenon known as the "likeability conundrum." Gender norms presume that women should be agreeable, warm, and nurturing. But when they violate these norms—such as when they step up to make a tough decision, share a strong opinion, or promote themselves—they're often penalized for that behavior in a way that men wouldn't be. We can all think of examples of women who have been publicly criticized for being "too aggressive" or called an "ice queen" or the "b word."

So how can you, as a woman, navigate this conundrum and develop a robust personal brand? Here are three strategies that can help ensure that your talents are recognized.

Network Both Inside and Outside Your Organization

Too many professionals overinvest in "bonding capital," to use a term popularized by Harvard sociologist Robert Putnam and underinvest in "bridging capital." In other words, they have too many connections who are like them (working in the same company or the same industry) and not nearly enough who are dissimilar.

When only a select group knows about your talents and abilities, you put yourself in jeopardy: You have fewer people who can speak to your contributions or provide support, whether that's help in securing additional resources for an important project or moving up to a new role. And if your department is reorganized or your company has layoffs, the people who understand your talents won't be in a position to help you.

Instead, consciously cultivate a broad network so that if your situation changes or you need backup, you have options. For instance, you could make a point of building professional connections with people you meet through hobbies, relationships of proximity (for instance, neighbors or parents at your kids' school), or friends of friends.

Control Your Narrative

We often assume that if we work hard, people will notice it over time. Or if we've made a transition, it will make intuitive sense to others. Because people are so overstretched these days, unfortunately that's almost never true. They're simply not paying close enough attention to us or our professional trajectory to formulate a coherent narrative for us. Worse, they may make in-accurate assumptions—that your skills must be wildly out of date since you took time off after having a child, or you shifted to functional roles because you were bored or "couldn't hack it"—which could cause you to miss out on growth opportunities.

Help others understand the truth about your journey by developing a clear and concise elevator pitch that explains how your previous skills connect with—and add value to—what you're doing now. Make that connection explicit, rather than hoping others will figure it out on their own.

To start, chart it out on paper. On one side, write down your past position or experience. On the other side, write down the job you currently hold. Then, find the connective tissue that links them.

For instance, your past might be "HR director" and your present might be "regional sales leader." An outsider may have no idea what connects these two positions and assume your career path is somewhat random. But you know that your experience in HR taught you about how to listen empathetically, understand what motivates people, and develop win-win solutions—all of which are perfect ingredients for sales success. When you're able to share this with others, they'll almost always get it and recognize the unique skills you bring to your position and the organization.

A crisp elevator pitch isn't just useful for times when you're job hunting. There are often opportunities to shape the way you're perceived by others—but most people miss them. For instance, new acquaintances will often ask how long you've been at your job, or how you came to your current field. Having a pithy answer ready means you can turn their question into an opportunity to subtly highlight your skills.

"I started out in HR and worked my way up to director," you might say. "But I became fascinated by the sales process and realized that the listening skills and ability to connect with people that I'd developed in HR would enable me to add real value to the company. So last year I transitioned into the role of head of Northeast sales." Here, you haven't just laid out your job titles: You've also provided context that conveys a strong personal brand.

Similarly, during performance reviews, you can make a point of reminding your boss about how you're leveraging key strengths you've developed over time. For instance, you could connect this year's increase in client upsells to your work developing your team's listening skills so they're more attuned to client needs.

Share Your Ideas Publicly

If you keep a low profile and let your work speak for itself, you may indeed develop a good reputation among the people you work closely with. But that's a relatively limited circle. Individuals in other departments or leaders many levels above you may not be aware of your contributions. And any staffing changes might disrupt the hard-fought reputational capital you've built. Your new boss or colleagues, who lack personal experience with you, may have no idea if you're any good or not.

Many women feel uncomfortable talking about their accomplishments and promoting themselves directly.

But there are other ways to showcase your areas of expertise when building a brand. Content creation is a good way to share your ideas and develop a positive reputation at scale. The precise mechanics will differ based on company policies (your ability to use social media may be limited in certain regulated industries, for instance), but in almost any organization there are ways that you can demonstrate your knowledge and help others.

For instance, you could volunteer to host a lunch-and-learn about a topic you've been researching, start writing for the company newsletter, or offer advice or respond to queries via the corporate intranet. Many professionals ignore these opportunities, assuming they're distractions that would take them away from their "real work," or they scoff that no one really uses these platforms anyway. Even if these tools aren't popular among your colleagues, higher-ups are almost always paying attention, since they view these channels as important vehicles for knowledge transfer and sharing best practices. One college friend of mine, for example, while working as a sales clerk at a large retailer, got into a private message exchange with the company CEO—eventually winning a trip to headquarters—as the result of one of her posts on the corporate intranet.

Content creation may also open up completely unexpected opportunities, including new jobs. Miranda Aisling Hynes, whom I profiled in my book *Stand Out*, used content creation in just this way. Hynes self-published a book about creativity that she gave to a friend who worked at an arts organization. He liked it and passed it along to his supervisor. When Hynes later applied for a job at the organization, she was a shoo-in because the book had already established her credibility in the field.

Personal branding is fraught for many professionals; no one wants to look like a craven self-promoter. And with the "likeability conundrum," building meaningful connections and a strong reputation at work is even more complicated for women.

But if we don't control our own narrative and show the world what we can contribute, odds are that very few people will actually notice. By following these strategies, you dramatically increase the odds that your true talents will get known, recognized, and appreciated.

––––––––––

Dorie Clark is a keynote speaker and an adjunct professor at Duke University's Fuqua School of Business. She is the author of *Reinventing You* (Harvard Business Review Press, 2013) and *Entrepreneurial You* (Harvard Business Review Press, 2017).

Communicate with Confidence

CHAPTER 4

How Women's Ways of Talking Differ from Men's

An interview with Deborah Tannen

Editor's note: Deborah Tannen was interviewed by HBR editors Amy Bernstein, Sarah Green Carmichael, and Nicole Torres.

Let's go back for a few minutes to the 1990s. More women were in the office, increasingly working alongside men or above them, not for them. Deborah Tannen, a Georgetown University linguistics professor, was concerned about these women being heard, given credit, and

---

Adapted from "Make Yourself Heard" on *Women at Work* (HBR podcast), January 24, 2018

accurately evaluated by their male colleagues and bosses. She knew from her research that the way women tend to talk at work can put them at a disadvantage—a topic that she described in her 1995 *Harvard Business Review* article, "The Power of Talk: Who Gets Heard and Why."

In this interview, Deborah Tannen discusses whether women still face the issue of being heard at work and how the way women speak may play a role in their being held back.

HBR: Has anything changed since you wrote in the 1990s about how women speak and are heard in the workplace?

Deborah Tannen: My impression is that not much has changed. I have been giving talks to various organizations, corporations, and companies pretty much nonstop since back then. And whenever I give these talks, I get the same response: "That's exactly what's happening to me. I experienced that just yesterday. You've just told the story of my life." That's the basis for my saying that not much has changed.

So, if women are still struggling to be heard for the same reasons today—if not much has changed—we want to get a better understanding of where that comes from. What's driving that?

I trace the way women and men tend to speak at work—and it's important to say "tend to," since nothing is true of all women or all men, and we have many influences on our styles other than our gender. But there are tendencies that girls and boys often learn as kids playing in same-sex groups. Girls tend to talk in ways that downplay their authority. If they play up the fact that they are the leaders in the group or that they're good at something, the other girls will criticize them: "She's bossy. She thinks she's something. She's stuck up." That's in contrast with the way boys tend to maintain their position in the group. They talk up what they're good at, maybe even making it into a game where they're trying to top each other. And the leader of the group is someone who tells the others what to do and gets it to stick. If we move into the workplace, a person in authority has to tell others what to do. And frequently, women will find ways to do it that don't seem too bossy, which downplays their authority. This can come across to others, especially to some men, as lacking or not deserving authority.

I was once speaking at a college and talking to the president of the school, and she told me of an experience she'd had. She had said to her assistant, "Could you do me a favor?" and then went on to ask her to do something. A member of the board took her aside and said, "Don't forget: You're the president." He had heard the fact that she'd started with "Could you do me a favor," as if she really thought she didn't have the authority to ask her own assistant to do something. In fact, you could see her way of asking as asserting authority. She knew the assistant had to do whatever she asked her to do, so she was saving face for the assistant by asking in a way that was, in her view, simply polite.

One of the ways I've noticed that women make not just requests but all kinds of leadership maneuvers less direct is by phrasing things as questions. You might hear a woman in a meeting say, "I'm not quite sure I'm following. Can someone recap for me?" if they think that the person running the meeting should have provided more detail or background but didn't in the beginning. Or, "Can someone please explain what the Q3 results mean?" even if they themselves know, but they think someone else in the group needs that information.

That's a great example of how women will often talk in ways that will save face for other people. And it's interpreted as something internal about them. (To see more examples of communication styles and how they're misinterpreted, see table 4-1.)

The narrative is usually that women are socialized to be less confident. But it seems like you're saying they're actually socialized to *sound* less confident.

Yes, absolutely. Laurie Heatherington, a psychology professor at Williams College, did a study where she asked hundreds of incoming freshmen at the university to predict the grades that they were going to get in their first year. There were two conditions. Half of them were asked to do it in a public way, either to orally tell the interviewer what grades they expected or write it on a piece of paper, and then those predictions were read aloud to a group. The

TABLE 4-1

Linguistic patterns and their consequences

This table shows examples of styles of talking *(including the* assumptions *behind each style) and* unintended consequences *a company may suffer because of misinterpreted stylistic differences.*

	Style of talking	Unintended consequences of style
Sharing credit	Uses "we" rather than "I" to describe accomplishments. *Why?* Using "I" seems too self-promoting.	Speaker doesn't get credit for accomplishments and may hesitate to offer good ideas in the future.
Acting modest	Downplays their certainty, rather than minimizing doubts, about future performance. *Why?* Confident behavior seems too boastful.	Speaker *appears* to lack confidence and, therefore, competence; others reject speaker's good ideas.
Asking questions	Asks questions freely. *Why?* Questions generate needed knowledge.	Speaker *appears* ignorant to others; if organization discourages speaker from asking questions, valuable knowledge remains buried.
Apologizing	Apologizes freely. *Why?* Apologies express concern for others.	Speaker *appears* to lack authority.
Giving feedback	Notes weaknesses only after first citing strengths. *Why?* Buffering criticism saves face for the individual receiving feedback.	Person receiving feedback concludes that areas needing improvement aren't important.
Avoiding verbal opposition	Avoids challenging others' ideas and hedges when stating own ideas. *Why?* Verbal opposition signals destructive fighting.	Others conclude that speaker has weak ideas.
Managing up	Avoids talking up achievements with higher-ups. *Why?* Emphasizing achievements to higher-ups constitutes boasting.	Managers conclude that speaker hasn't achieved much and doesn't deserve recognition or promotion.
Being indirect	Speaks indirectly rather than bluntly when telling subordinates what to do. *Why?* Blatantly directing others is too bossy.	Superiors conclude that manager lacks confidence or competence, and subordinates may judge her directives as unimportant or not urgent.

Source: Adapted from Deborah Tannen, "The Power of Talk: Who Gets Heard and Why," *Harvard Business Review,* September–October 1995 (product #95510)

other was private: Write what you expect, close it in an envelope, seal up the envelope, and no one's going to see it. In the conditions where their predictions were public, women predicted much lower grades for themselves than men tended to. When their predictions were private, the results were pretty much the same for the women and the men. The women were downplaying what they really expected so that they wouldn't come across as too full of themselves.

There might be something a little bit different going on with credit taking and women, where for some of us, taking credit is kind of a repugnant act. Have you seen anything on that front?

Yes. I observed that women frequently said "we" when talking about something they personally had done or accomplished. I also observed men saying "I" about things that they were not individually, personally responsible for. And I think that has a lot do with our sense of what's appropriate. A lot of women feel it's kind of boastful to say "I." The word should be avoided. So, they'll say "we" to be gracious about the people they work with. But they assume other people will know that they really did it. And that's similar to a more general pattern by which many women felt: *If I do a good job, it will be noticed. I don't have to call attention to what I've done.* Whereas many men realize that they should call attention to their work or people won't know.

A lot of these ways of speaking that women have taken for granted or assume are appropriate are realistic. It's a phenomenon I often refer to as a double bind: a situation in which you must fulfill two requirements, but anything you do to fulfill one violates the other. Women in positions of authority must fulfill expectations for a good woman and those for a good leader. But those expectations are mutually exclusive. If she speaks as we expect women to speak—be self-effacing, downplaying her accomplishments—she will be liked but seen as less competent and confident than she really is. If a female leader speaks as we expect a person in authority to speak, she may be respected but not liked and seen as too aggressive. It's a challenge to find some middle ground.

What does it sound like to successfully navigate that?

I'll give an example. A woman has to tell a subordinate to do something. She could ask, "Do you think you could do this by 4:00?" Here, the question form, the high pitch, the rising annotation, all of that would be considerate and not too imposing. People would like her but see her as lacking authority. She could say, "Do this by 4:00." That would be authoritative but might come across as too assertive for a woman. Or she could say, "I need this by 4:00. Do you think you could do that?" So, it's something in between the very self-effacing and the very declarative.

There are also conversational rituals that women have, such as apologizing when something's not their fault, simply because something bad happened. Or ritualistically complimenting other people, especially other women. But sometimes these rituals are left uncompleted by the other party, making it awkward for the women.

Here's an example of a conversation ritual that can backfire when the other person doesn't do their part. Women are often told they apologize too much. They're told, "Don't apologize; it's not your fault." Sometimes a woman will use an apology to get the other person to apologize. For instance, let's say there was a meeting, and you're the boss. Your subordinate didn't come to the meeting, but they were supposed to be there. You might say something like, "Gee, sorry you weren't at the meeting. If I forgot to tell you about it, I'm sorry, it was really pretty important." She knows she told him about the meeting. She has apologized for A; he is supposed to apologize for B.

So he should say—and she would expect him to say—"Oh, yeah, you did tell me. I'm sorry, something came up, and I couldn't make it. But I'll make sure to find out what went on, and it won't happen again." If he says, "Yeah, make sure you tell me next time," it's like sitting on a seesaw or a teeter-totter. You sit on your side, and you trust the other person to sit on their side. If they get off, you go plopping to the ground, and you wonder how you got there. But it really wasn't anything you did. The other person did not do their part of the conversational ritual.

If conversational rituals have changed because there are more women in the workplace and more female leaders, and they introduce their own conversational rituals— there's more complimenting, more apologizing going on, maybe—why aren't those behaviors or rituals more valued if they're more common?

When I did this research back in the early nineties, I was quite convinced that when there were more women in the workplace, the standards would change. So, in a way, I'm disappointed and also surprised that they haven't. The explanation I would surmise is that a sense of how a person in authority should speak or behave is still based on an image of a man in authority. We still associate authority with men. Sadly, the double bind is alive and well.

Deborah Tannen is university professor and professor of linguistics at Georgetown University in Washington, D.C. She is the author of 12 books, including *You Just Don't Understand: Women and Men in Conversation*, which introduced to the general public the idea of female and male styles of communication, and *Talking from 9 to 5: Women and Men at Work*, on which her 1995 *Harvard Business Review* article is based. Her most recent book is *You're the Only One I Can Tell: Inside the Language of Women's Friendships*.

CHAPTER 5

Women, Find Your Voice

by Kathryn Heath, Jill Flynn, and Mary Davis Holt

A senior manager is asked to give up an executive committee seat because the CEO wants to shrink the group's size and plans to retain only "the most engaged" members.

The leader of a $50 million division is passed over for promotion to the C-suite after failing to fully participate in strategic discussions in which "you have to shout to be heard."

A marketing executive is surprised when a colleague drops by after a meeting with this advice: "Stop acting like a facilitator. Start saying what you stand for."

Reprinted from *Harvard Business Review*, June 2014 (product #R1406K)

The people described above have several things in common. They are all successful and ambitious. They are all admired by colleagues and superiors. Yet they have all failed to assert themselves in high-level meetings. And they are all women.

Our research reveals that such stories are typical. During decades of leadership coaching, we have consistently heard women say that they feel less effective in meetings than they do in other business situations. Some say that their voices are ignored or drowned out. Others tell us that they can't find a way into the conversation. Their male colleagues and managers have witnessed the phenomenon. In fact, several men reported seeing a female colleague get rattled or remain silent even when she was the expert at the table.

In 2012 we decided to take a systematic look at the issue. We began by examining 360-degree feedback we'd collected on 1,100 female executives at or above the vice president level—more than 7,000 surveys in all. We found widespread evidence in the executives' comments and in those of their colleagues and managers that meetings were a big stumbling block. To corroborate and update what we saw in the 360s, we surveyed 270 female managers in *Fortune* 500 organizations. More than half reported that meetings were a significant issue or a "work in progress." Finally, to get a picture of how the gender divide plays out in the highest-level meetings, we interviewed 65 top executives, including both male and female CEOs, from companies such as JPMorgan Chase, McDonald's, PepsiCo, Lowe's, Time Warner, and eBay. In all our investigations, we found that men and women generally agreed on the problems but often disagreed on their causes.

Although we have focused exclusively on women, we believe that many of our findings apply to others as well—members of racial and ethnic minorities and men with more-reserved personalities. We also realize that some women don't fit the mold we describe. However, we believe that our research and advice will be useful to the many female managers who do struggle in critical meetings. We think it can also help bosses keen to encourage all team members, male and female, to contribute to their full potential.

What Men See

The male managers we interviewed were well aware that women often have a hard time making their otherwise strong voices heard in meetings, either because they're not speaking loudly enough or because they can't find a way to break into the conversation at all. More than a third indicated that when their female peers do speak up, they fail to articulate a strong point of view. Half said that women allow themselves to be interrupted, apologize repeatedly, and fail to back up opinions with evidence. One male executive offered this description of two "highly successful and powerful" female colleagues in a meeting he attended: "One went off on tangents, bringing in disparate points with few facts. It was like a snowball going down a hill and picking up stuff in its path. The other got wrapped up in the passion she feels for the topic, and she said the same thing three different ways."

Men frequently described women as being defensive when challenged and apt to panic or freeze if they lose the attention of the room. "These are high-octane meetings that are filled with domineering personalities," one CEO told us. "Women are often either quiet and tentative, or they pipe up at the wrong moment, and it sounds more like noise to some of us."

What Women Feel

If men perceive that women lack confidence at meetings, it's because in many cases they do. Female executives, vastly outnumbered in boardrooms and C-suites and with few role models and sponsors, report feeling alone, unsupported, outside their comfort zones, and unable to advocate forcefully for their perspectives in many high-level meetings. As one said, "It is harder to read the room if there are no other women around the table."

Many women admitted that they do get rattled when they're challenged. In fact, they're uncomfortable with conflict in general. They find it unsettling when anyone receives a sharp public rebuke, and they often brood and second-guess themselves long after meetings are over. They don't see themselves as defensive on their own account, though they report feeling empathy for others, and perhaps an occasional touch of anger. "When men dismiss women," said a female vice president, "women may interpret it as being 'put in their place.'"

Most say that the trouble they have articulating their views has more to do with timing than with their ability to marshal facts, stick to a point, or control their feelings. In coaching sessions, women have told us that they sometimes get lukewarm responses when they raise an opposing view after the group has started to cohere around an idea. But they are strongly opposed to simply repeating others' ideas in different words, something they feel many of their male colleagues do.

"Men have a way to neatly repackage ideas," says Lynne Ford, executive vice president and head of distribution at Calvert Investments. "They restate and amplify what you just said." Even as she acknowledges that she has seen this tactic used very effectively, she adds, "It's gamesmanship."

What Women Can Do

In the future, when more women are leading organizations, they can approach meetings in a way that feels perfectly natural to them. In the meantime, several practical steps can help them become more effective and more comfortable.

Master the "pre-meeting"

Our research shows that female executives are very efficient. They come to meetings on time. They leave as soon as the last agenda item has been completed, rushing off to the next meeting or heading back to their offices to put out fires. We've found that men are more likely to spend time connecting with one another to test their ideas and garner support. They arrive at meetings early in order to get a good seat and chat with colleagues, and they stay afterward to close off the discussion and talk about other issues on their minds.

Women could go a long way toward addressing the problem of timing and their feelings of isolation if they sounded out colleagues and built allies in this way. They need to get in on what several men described as the "meetings before the meetings," where much of the real work happens. Participating in these informal advance conversations can help clarify the true purpose of a meeting, making it much easier to take an active part in the conversation. Will the group be asked to make a decision? Confirm a consensus? Establish power? It's often not apparent in the official agenda.

"Men are really good at the pre-meeting," said a male senior vice president. "This is their preparation."

Prepare to speak

Many women we talked with prefer to pitch their ideas in formal presentations rather than in the more conversational way many men favor. Our advice to female executives, as counterintuitive as it sounds, is: *Prepare* to speak spontaneously. "You need to have written down some things you want to talk about," Ford says. "Even some of the casual, off-the-cuff remarks you hear have been rehearsed. If it sounds good, it was probably prepared."

Women who do their homework and come to a meeting with an accurate sense of what it's really about and how it will probably unfold can build on others' remarks. Being armed with some cogent comments or questions can allow them to move the conversation forward. Anne Taylor, vice chairman and regional managing partner at Deloitte LLP, says she has the most impact in a meeting when she finds an opportunity to "turn it in a different and more productive direction with questions like, "Have you thought of this . . . ?" or "What if we looked at it this way . . . ?"

MAKE YOUR LANGUAGE MORE MUSCULAR

Male executives we interviewed said that in order to hold the floor in meetings, they use active words and authoritative statements, avoid hedging, take ownership of their opinions, and build on others' ideas instead of just agreeing with them. Here are some ways in which women can follow suit.

Instead of this	Use this
How about . . . ?	I strongly suggest . . .
I tend to agree.	That is absolutely right, and here's why . . .
I think maybe . . .	My strong advice is . . .
I agree.	I agree completely, because . . .
Maybe we can . . .	Here is my plan . . .
Well, what if . . . ?	I recommend . . .

When the conversation advances rapidly, holding the floor requires the use of "muscular words," as one male executive put it—active, authoritative, precise language that shows you're taking ownership of your opinions (see the sidebar "Make Your Language More Muscular").

Keep an even keel

"Passion is a key component of persuasion," says eBay senior vice president Steve Boehm. "The question is, "How passionate can women be?" That is, how much feeling can they safely express?

Realistically, our research suggests, the answer is "not very much." In our 360-degree feedback survey analysis, we learned that when women said they felt "passionate" about an idea or an opinion, their male managers and colleagues often perceived "too much emotion."

Men acknowledge the existence of a double standard. "Women have to be mindful to stay within the guardrails; men don't," one male executive told us. Until that changes, women need to ensure that they are seen as composed and in command of their emotions. It is not so much *what* women say as *how* they say it. They need to keep an even tone, not shift to a higher pitch when under duress. They need to speak deliberately and avoid signaling frustration through sarcasm or curtness.

HE SAID, SHE SAID

In interviews and written comments, men acknowledged that women often struggle to make themselves heard at meetings, but they didn't always agree with their female peers about the reasons.

He said	She said
We're afraid of how women will react to criticism.	We don't get feedback, even when we ask for it.
Women need to be concise and remain on point.	We don't like to repackage old ideas or restate the obvious.
Women need a stronger point of view.	It's difficult to get a word in.
Women need to speak informally and off the cuff.	We like to put together presentations.
Women get defensive when they are challenged.	We obsess about a meeting for days after it's over.
Women are more emotional than men.	It's not emotion—it's passion.
Women are less confident than men.	Yes, but we're outnumbered five to one, and we tend to feel less fully "at the table."

Women must also learn to move past confrontation without taking it personally. Karen Dahut, executive vice president at Booz Allen Hamilton, offers this learning experience: "I put out some controversial points in an executive committee meeting a while back, which we debated for a good while. Eventually I realized we could go no further, so I closed the conversation. But I thought about the disagreement all weekend. I worried I'd harmed my work relationships. I wondered what it would take to get them back. On Monday I saw some of my male colleagues—and there was no problem. To them, it was nothing!"

A little compartmentalization can be useful here. As one male senior executive put it, "Men can be intense and challenging, but then we go out and get a beer together."

What Organizations Can Do

Women can certainly do a better job of speaking up in meetings, but bosses can also help ensure that women's voices are heard.

First, companies should fix broken feedback mechanisms. Fully 68% of the women in our study said they seldom receive any direct feedback about their meeting behavior. One male executive admitted, "We talk *about* them, but not *to* them." Managers need to overcome their reluctance about giving direct feedback on this area of development issues.

Next, at the risk of stating the obvious, leaders need to invite more women to the table. When a woman walks into a meeting and finds that only two of the 15 people present are women, it takes a toll. Peer support and role models make a difference.

Finally, bosses need to proactively pull women into the conversation. During our interviews, we asked 30 high-ranking women to name the one thing they would change about how men treat them in meetings. Thirty-eight percent said, "Ask us direct questions" or "Bring us into the discussion."

These changes can have profound results. "Eighteen years ago a male colleague [who] had been in a series of meetings with me recognized that I had something to say but was uncomfortable speaking out," a female executive vice president told us. "One day he looked at all the guys around the table. He said he knew I had a point, and he would like me to just say it and not to worry about how it might be received. He got the guys . . . to make it a safe environment for me to speak. I have been speaking up ever since."

Kathryn Heath is a partner at Flynn Heath Holt Leadership, which specializes in leadership development programs and executive coaching for women. She is a coauthor of *The Influence Effect: A New Path to Power for Women*. **Jill Flynn** is a partner at Flynn Heath Holt Leadership and a coauthor of *Break Your Own Rules: How to Change the Patterns of Thinking That Block Women's Paths to Power*. **Mary Davis Holt, MBA,** is a senior consultant with Flynn Heath Holt Leadership, and she is a coauthor of *Break Your Own Rules: How to Change the Patterns of Thinking That Block Women's Paths to Power*. Follow them on Twitter @FlynnHeathHolt.

CHAPTER 6

Show Passion at Work Without Seeming "Emotional"

by Kathryn Heath and Jill Flynn

One of our coaching clients, a VP at a consumer products company, was abruptly silenced when she tried to make a point at a recent executive committee meeting. The problem? She was passionate—and it didn't go over well.

Sales at the organization had plummeted, and the group was discussing the efficacy of its newest product. Our executive, Claudia, was convinced that the sales

---

Adapted from "How Women Can Show Passion at Work Without Seeming 'Emotional'" on hbr.org, September 30, 2015 (product #H02DNV)

team needed to be examined instead. So she spoke up: "Our reps are apathetic and underperforming. They don't have what they need to close deals. We should make some major changes *right now*, or we'll lose the year." She found herself speaking loudly and gesturing with her hands for effect. But when she stopped to take a breath, she looked around the table and saw mostly blank stares. As she geared up to elaborate, a male colleague sitting across from her waved his hand across his throat like a movie director cutting a scene. He shut her down and re-directed the conversation back to the product.

Claudia was furious. After the meeting, she confronted her colleague. He apologized for cutting her off but told her she had "reacted with too much emotion." He said, "You were off point, and your tone seemed excited and inappropriate." That's not the way Claudia saw the situation. She walked away wondering, "Where is the line between appropriate passion and too much emotion?"

It's a recurring theme in our coaching sessions with women. Although passion has a legitimate place in business, it can be misinterpreted—especially when women are doing the communicating and male colleagues are on the receiving end. That's what we've found in our review of more than 1,000 360-degree feedback reports on female executives. When women fervently sell an idea or argue against the consensus, for example, we've seen that male colleagues or managers say things like, "She was too hyped up" and "She was emotional," whereas the women themselves say they were simply advancing their cause or expressing an opinion, albeit passionately.

This lines up with what we've found in our qualitative research. In interviews on how women can find their voice in meetings, female executives told us they worry that their comments during heated discussions are misinterpreted as emotional. One of their pain points is that they are perceived as "overly direct," and they often "have to reword or reposition" what they say. One executive reported that her passion was met "with great silence," and she asked, "Is that my gender or my communication style?"

The answer is both, of course, because her style—passionate expression—is viewed differently by men and women. In our research, overall, male executives shared "an ongoing perception that women are more emotional than men," and they largely felt that women "need to be aware of it and remain composed." We also heard from men that unchecked emotion by women makes their ideas less convincing and compromises their credibility, because it focuses attention on style rather than content.

That's not to say that women are in the wrong. It's a "lost in translation" issue, with repercussions for men and women alike. If male managers don't check their biases and those of their colleagues—and adjust how they receive and filter information from women—they will miss crucial input, and their decision quality may suffer.

For women, matters of perception are tricky, but here are some things you can do to minimize miscommunication and put your passion to work for you.

Be intentional

If you use your passion to make a point, do so deliberately as opposed to in the moment. How? Plan your argument in advance and generate support before meetings so your passion won't take others by surprise. We also tell women to use language that is passionate but a tone that's moderate. In other words, remain in control so that people focus on the content of your argument and take it seriously.

Know your audience

Claudia's executive committee was stacked with number crunchers and business analysts. She acknowledges, in retrospect, that they are swayed more readily by figures than by pure debate. She might have held the floor longer if she had begun her remarks with quantitative facts. For instance: "The sales numbers are down 6% this quarter, so let's start by examining the sales strategy. Here's what I have in mind."

Use other tools of influence

Combining passion with logic, specificity, creativity, and experience can be more effective than relying on passion alone. If some colleagues, male or female, don't respond to passionate appeals, they may respond more favorably to a different tactic. In addition, the versatility signals that you are in control of your emotions and able to switch gears in order to effectively make a point.

Support what your gut is telling you

If you feel passionate about something, say it proudly and then proceed to back up your feelings with facts. The people around you are more likely to be swayed by your open declaration if it's clear that you have reason and logic on your side. They might even find your passion contagious.

It can be tough striking the right balance between what others see as emotion and you see as passion. But by following the four tips outlined here, you can use your own strong feelings to be more persuasive and influential at work.

Kathryn Heath is a partner at Flynn Heath Holt Leadership, which specializes in leadership development programs and executive coaching for women. She is a coauthor of *The Influence Effect: A New Path to Power for Women*. **Jill Flynn** is a partner at Flynn Heath Holt Leadership and a coauthor of *Break Your Own Rules: How to Change the Patterns of Thinking That Block Women's Paths to Power*. Follow them on Twitter @FlynnHeathHolt.

CHAPTER 7

To Seem Confident, You Must Be Seen as Warm

by Margarita Mayo

Why are there so few women in leadership roles? As we've read throughout the book, one frequently cited reason has to do with confidence—whether that reason is accurate or not. For instance, in a 2012 study my colleagues and I found that women tend to rate their abilities accurately, while men tend to be overconfident about theirs.[1] Thus, one argument goes, women are less confident than men, which hurts their chances of promotion.

Adapted from "To Seem Confident, Women Have to Be Seen as Warm" on hbr.org, July 8, 2016 (product #H03036)

Previous studies have measured how women see themselves. But my research collaborators, Laura Guillen of ESMT and Natalia Karelaia of INSEAD, and I wanted to know how outside perceivers such as bosses, subordinates, and colleagues rate women's confidence, and what influences those ratings.

Psychology professor Susan Fiske of Princeton University and her colleagues have shown that people seem to universally use two dimensions to judge others: competence and warmth.[2] We decided to test for both of those factors in addition to confidence. As a proxy for the likelihood of being promoted, we also tested for influence, on the theory that people who are seen as influential are more likely to move up to leadership roles.

We conducted a study analyzing the judgments that colleagues made regarding the competence and warmth of 236 engineers working in project teams at a multinational software development company. As part of their performance assessment, the engineers were confidentially evaluated online by their supervisor, peers, and collaborators on competence and warmth. A total of 810 raters provided the evaluation. A year later, we collected a second wave of data on the same 236 engineers about their apparent confidence at work and their influence in the organization. This time, a total of 1,236 raters provided information.

Our study shows that men are seen as confident if they are seen as competent, but women are seen as confident only if they come across as both competent and warm. Women must be seen as warm in order to capitalize on their competence and be seen as confident and influential at work; competent men are seen as confident and influential whether they are warm or not.

In other words, for male engineers, competence and perceived confidence go hand in hand. The more competent male engineers are, the more confident they are seen as being (and vice versa). The more confident they are seen as being, the more influence they have in the organization, regardless of whether others like them. It seems that warmth is irrelevant to men appearing confident and influential, at least when they are performing a typically male job like engineering.

For women, in the absence of warmth there was virtually no relationship between competence and confidence ratings. When women were seen as both warm and competent, they were also seen as more confident—and thus more influential. Competent but less-affable female engineers were evaluated by their colleagues as less confident in their professional roles. These female engineers were, in turn, less influential within the organization. In sum, women's professional performance is not evaluated independent from their personal warmth.

Personal experience and empirical research suggest that it's not enough for women to be merely as gregarious, easygoing, sociable, and helpful as men. To get credit for being warm—and to have their other strengths recognized—they might need to be even more so. (See the sidebar "How to Convey Warmth.")

I still remember my first performance evaluation as an assistant lecturer: I was told to be more "nurturing." I had gone to just as many social events as the men had, had been just as gregarious with my students. But

HOW TO CONVEY WARMTH

by Heidi Grant

Many people think they project warmth but in fact don't. Fortunately there are some very simple things you can do to convey warmth when interacting with others.

First, maintain eye contact, particularly when other people are talking. A lot of us know that eye contact is important for looking confident. But actually, when other people are talking, it's critical that you look at them because that's a clear signal of interest.

I know a lot of people who don't do this. Even though they are listening, they'll let their eyes wander around the room, and that gives a very clear signal that they're not listening.

It's also important to nod when someone is talking. That's another subtle way to indicate that you're paying attention and that you're understanding what someone is saying. It's strange when you get into a conversation with someone who doesn't nod. You immediately feel frostiness and tension. You may not be able to put your finger on what it is, but what you're sensing is that lack of affirmation, that lack of a signal that says, "Hey, I'm paying attention to you. I'm listening to you and I understand."

Affirmations, in general, are very important. That's a word that people associate with *Saturday Night Live* character Stuart Smalley or saying, "I like myself." But affirmations are really just simple expressions that we use to say things like, "Well, that must have been difficult for you" or "Oh, I understand," asking questions about a person, or asking them to talk about themselves. These are all are indicators of warmth.

It's important not only to try to do more of these things but also to ask people you trust to tell you whether or not you do them. One thing I found again and again is that often I'd talk to people about these behaviors and they'd say, "Oh, yeah, I do that." And then often, if it's a friend of mine, I can say, "No, you actually don't. That's why I'm telling you that this is something you need to do more of."

Ask people who you trust to tell you the truth. "Do I give off signals that indicate that I'm not listening?" They might tell you, "Yeah, if I didn't know you better, I would think you were kind of a jerk." They've come to know over time that you actually are warmer than you appear. But you really want to make sure you are appearing as warm as you are. That's why it's so important to focus on particular behaviors that we know actually send the right signals.

Heidi Grant, PhD, is a senior scientist at the Neuroleadership Institute and the associate director for the Motivation Science Center at Columbia University. She is the author of the best-selling *Nine Things Successful*

(*continued*)

HOW TO CONVEY WARMTH

(*continued*)

People Do Differently (Harvard Business Review Press, 2012). Her most recent book is *No One Understands You and What to Do About It* (Harvard Business Review Press, 2015), which has been featured in national and international media. Follow her on Twitter @heidgrantphd.

Adapted from "Understand How People See You" on *HBR IdeaCast* (podcast), April 16, 2015

women are simply expected to show more warmth. Studies show, for example, that women's performance reviews contain nearly twice as much language about being warm, empathetic, helpful, and dedicated to others.[3]

Our study suggests that if women are to succeed in a biased world, encouraging them to be more confident is not enough. To get credit for having confidence and competence, and to have the influence in their organizations that they want to have, women must go out of their way to be seen as warm.

My colleagues and I wish this weren't the case. We wish women and men could both be evaluated on merit. But as our research shows, we seem to be a long way off from that reality.

***

Margarita Mayo is a professor of leadership and organizational behavior at IE Business School in Madrid.

She was featured on the Thinkers50 Radar as one of 30 thought leaders to watch in 2017. She is the author of *Yours Truly: Staying Authentic in Leadership and Life.*

NOTES

1. Margarita Mayo et al., "Aligning or Inflating Your Leadership Self-Image? Longitudinal Study of Responses to Peer Feedback in MBA Teams," *Academy of Management Learning & Education* 11, no. 4 (2012): 631–652.

2. Susan T. Fiske, Amy J. C. Cuddy, and Peter Glick, "Universal Dimensions of Social Cognition: Warmth and Competence," *Trends in Cognitive Sciences* 11, no. 2 (2006): 77–83.

3. Shelley Correll and Caroline Simard, "Research: Vague Feedback Is Holding Women Back," hbr.org, April 29, 2016 (product #H02UUL).

Build a Network of Support

CHAPTER 8

Three Ways Women Can Rethink Office Politics

by Kathryn Heath

Men and women don't look at office politics and power dynamics the same way. That's what my consulting partners and I found when we surveyed 134 senior executives in large organizations and conducted follow-up interviews with 44 of them. There's no right or wrong here, but the discrepancies help explain why women assert themselves differently.

We found that men tend to talk about "competition" when they describe office politics, using language like

---

Adapted from "3 Simple Ways for Women to Rethink Office Politics and Wield More Influence at Work" on hbr.org, December 18, 2017 (product #H042FL)

"the tools people use to win at work," whereas women are more likely to cast it as "a natural part of influencing" and emphasize the ability to shape "ideas and agendas." Similarly, women and men report having different *objectives* in the political situations they face at work. Men use words like "achieving results," and women—again and again—talk about "influencing others."

Such differences are likely fueled in part by lingering double binds and gender biases in the workplace. In our study, 81% of women and 66% of men said that women are judged more harshly than men when they are seen as "engaging in corporate politics." So women don't want to be viewed as political—it undermines them. That may explain why 68% of women said they dislike office politics, even though they want to assert themselves at work—and why the majority of women in our interviews said they were more interested in "influence" than in pure power.

Like everything else, authentic influence takes practice: You train so you can transform. Here are a few strategies we've seen work for the women we've coached.

Create Relationship Maps

Step one is knowing which people to influence. Who has decision-making power in your organization? Who are the informal influencers? Who is most likely to resist your agenda because of competing objectives?

Creating a relationship map can help you sort all of this out. People in sales close deals by identifying deal advocates and blockers, often using complex software and customer databases to generate the relationship maps they need. For our purposes, the only prop required is a legal pad, a whiteboard, or a laptop. Your relationship map can look like an annotated org chart or a more complicated networking diagram. The key is to identify the stakeholders and influencers who can help you achieve your job and career goals. This visual exercise allows you to cultivate a deeper understanding of your network so you can build meaningful connections and secure allies to amplify your influence. Women are generally good at relationships (the Gallup survey "Women in America: Work and Life Well-Lived," shows this), and they can use this strength to study their maps and build bridges to decision makers.

Construct a Scaffolding

We can scale our influence by adding multiple layers of support—not only the usual mentors and senior-level sponsors, but also "agents" and "truth tellers."

Agents are people in your organization or industry with whom you are close. Ideally, they already appreciate and trust you enough to vouch for your talent and promote you to others. They don't require as much effort to cultivate as mentors and sponsors (both of which we'll discuss later in this section), but they require nurturing. Your very best agents proactively look for opportunities to help you by mentioning your name in key conversations and sharing intelligence.

Truth tellers are exactly what they sound like: the trusted allies who tell it like it is. They look you in the eye when you are up for a promotion and say, "If you don't work at gaining more followership, you may miss your chance to move up." Or, after a crucial presentation: "It went well, but next time make stronger eye contact, speak slowly, and use muscular language."

Start your scaffolding with a small, manageable number of diverse advocates, and build it up over time.

Think Bigger

Finally, don't doubt your ability to wield influence. Are systemic barriers still stacked against us? Yes. But accumulating influence requires big, bold ideas. So we coach women executives to think bigger, aim higher, and own their vision.

As one female executive told us: "I have made it my mission to show up with confidence and to be my true self. I have found that influence and authenticity are inextricably linked. Only by being truly self-confident can we influence others to follow us."

Kathryn Heath is a partner at Flynn Heath Holt Leadership, which specializes in leadership development programs and executive coaching for women. She is a coauthor of *The Influence Effect: A New Path to Power for Women*. Follow her on Twitter @FlynnHeathHolt.

CHAPTER 9

You Need Many Mentors, Not Just One

by Dorie Clark

These days everyone knows that finding a mentor is valuable. But it's increasingly rare that we actually have one. For instance, in an in-depth study of professional service firms, Harvard Business School professor Thomas DeLong and his colleagues discovered that "Everyone we spoke with over age 40 could name a mentor in his or her professional life, but younger people often could not."[1] They continued, "Junior professionals joining a firm 20 years ago could count on the partners treating

---

Adapted from "Your Career Needs Many Mentors, Not Just One" on hbr.org, January 19, 2017 (product #H03EOA)

them like protégés." Today, job turnover, layoffs, and increased bottom-line pressures have taken a hatchet to that implicit agreement. The answer isn't to give up on finding a mentor, however—it's to broaden our search.

Many professionals have had success with creating mastermind groups, which are a curated mix of peers who meet regularly to discuss professional challenges and hold one another accountable. But less formal arrangements—sometimes called a mentor board of directors, a personal board of directors, or a kitchen cabinet—can also be effective.

The chief distinction between finding a mentor and creating a mentor board of directors is that there is less pressure to find one person who represents your ideal future self. You can diversify your search criteria and learn from a variety of people. It also allows you to look beyond the classic notion of a mentor as someone who is older and wiser than you.

Mentors can even be our juniors—by decades. Take Hank Phillippi Ryan, an Emmy-winning investigative reporter I profiled in my book *Reinventing You*. She launched an award-winning side career as a mystery author after being inspired by a former intern of hers who had penned a novel. "It was percolating in my head," she told me. "If she can write a book, I can write a book." In order to form your own mentor board of directors— stocked with an assortment of talented peers, senior professionals, and junior colleagues—keep the following questions in mind.

What Do You Want to Learn?

The first step in developing your board is a rigorous self-assessment. Where are you headed professionally, and what skills do you need in order to get there? If you're planning to shift functional roles—from sales to HR, for instance—you may want to seek out a mentor with HR experience. Similarly, if you intend to move up the management ranks, finding a mentor with great delegation skills or the ability to build relationships with difficult employees could be valuable. And don't forget about personal qualities in addition to tactical skills. The biggest game changer for you professionally may be cultivating more patience or more humility; you can seek out role models in those areas as well.

Whom Do You Respect Most?

Once you've developed your list of skills, write down the people you know and respect who possess them. Think broadly: They could be peers, senior leaders, or even (like Phillippi Ryan's mentor) interns or junior employees. Once, when I was giving a talk on mentorship at a prominent law firm, a partner shared that early in her career, her secretary was her mentor, because the secretary, who had been at the firm for decades, understood the business's office politics and taught her to stand up for herself. It's also useful to cast a wide net outside the office. At another mentorship workshop I conducted, one leader said that her yoga teacher was a mentor because the woman helped remind her about work-life balance.

How Can You Spend More Time with Them?

Identifying your mentor board of directors is great, but it's all hypothetical unless you actually make an effort to spend more time learning from them. For each person, think through how and when you'll make time to connect. With some of the mentors, like work colleagues, the opportunities may be plentiful. For others—a grad school professor or a former coworker who has moved to another company—you may need to think creatively. Could you invite them for a monthly lunch? Call them periodically to check in during your drive home? Arrange to meet up at a conference you'll both be attending? For each person, the opportunities (and what feels appropriate) will differ. Make a list, and write down specific strategies.

How Can You Make the Relationship Reciprocal?

As with any mentor or sponsor relationship, you need to make yourself valuable in return. For each person on your list, think about what skills or qualities *you* bring to the table and may be able to offer them. For instance, if you're adept at social media, you could offer to help a senior professional tune up his LinkedIn profile (if he's expressed a desire to do so). Or you may have skills outside of work that your mentors value—anything from restaurant recommendations to fitness tips. For these relationships to endure, it's important to make sure they're reciprocal. That way, you're learning from each other rather than imposing on one another's time (or worrying that you're doing so).

Professional success requires a myriad of skills, knowledge, and abilities, more than we could ever hope to learn on our own. That's why mentors who can help us improve are so critical. Archetypal mentors—beneficent, all-knowing senior professionals—are in short supply these days. By updating our notions of mentorship and building a mentor board of directors, we can benefit from the knowledge of talented colleagues all around us.

Dorie Clark is a keynote speaker and an adjunct professor at Duke University's Fuqua School of Business. She is the author of *Reinventing You* (Harvard Business Review Press, 2013) and *Entrepreneurial You* (Harvard Business Review Press, 2017).

NOTE

1. Thomas J. DeLong, John J. Gabarro, and Robert J. Lees, "Why Mentoring Matters in a Hypercompetitive World," *Harvard Business Review*, January 2008 (product #R0801H).

CHAPTER 10

The Right Way to Find a Career Sponsor

by Sylvia Ann Hewlett

As part of her employer's mentoring program, every month Willa meets one-on-one with Joan, a former executive vice president at the global financial services firm where they both work. Warm and nurturing, Joan is a tireless champion of working mothers like Willa, having herself negotiated a flex arrangement working out of her home in Connecticut while overseeing operations in India.

Joan is unquestionably Willa's role model as well as mentor. But is she the senior leader best positioned to

---

Adapted from content posted on hbr.org, September 11, 2013 (product #H00B7X)

get Willa promoted to her dream job of heading up M&A at corporate headquarters? Probably not.

As sympathetic confidants, mentors can't be beat. They listen to your issues, offer advice, and review approaches to solving problems. The whole idea of having a mentor (or a few) is to discuss what you cannot or dare not bring up with your boss or colleagues. But when it comes to powering your career up to corporate heights, you need a sponsor. As I explain in my book, *Forget a Mentor, Find a Sponsor*, sponsors may advise or steer you, but their chief role is to develop you as a leader. Why? Not so much from like-mindedness or altruism, but because furthering *your* career helps further *their* career, organization, or vision. (See the sidebar "What Do *You* Bring to the Table?") Where a mentor might help you envision your next position, a sponsor will advocate for your promotion and lever open the door. Sponsorship doesn't rig the game; on the contrary, it ensures you get what you deserve—and can propel your career much farther than mentors alone can.

When scanning the horizon for would-be sponsors—and yes, you need more than one—many high-potential women make the mistake of focusing on role models rather than powerfully positioned sponsors. My research shows that they align themselves with people whom they trust and like or who, they believe, trust and like them. According to survey data from the Center for Talent Innovation, 49% of women in the "marzipan layer," that talent-rich band just under the executive level, search for support among those "whose leadership style I admire." What style is that? Forty-two percent are looking

WHAT DO *YOU* BRING TO THE TABLE?

Just as you would with a mentor, you want to make sure your sponsorship relationship is reciprocal. Show your sponsor what skills or qualities you provide and how you can help advance their vision or career.

Some protégés add value through their technical expertise or social media savvy. Others derive an enduring identity through fluency in another language or culture. Consider acquiring skills that your job doesn't mandate but that set you apart and make you a stronger contributor to a team. For example, Genpact CEO Tiger Tyagarajan had a special ability to build teams from scratch and coach raw talent—an invaluable asset that was key as the firm transitioned from a startup into a multinational info-tech giant. One 25-year-old sales rep, noting that her potential sponsor "wasn't exactly current in terms of the internet," took pains to brief her on job candidates whose résumés bristled with technical jargon and references to social media innovation that she simply couldn't understand, let alone assess for relevance. "I just helped educate her so she didn't come off as some kind of dinosaur," says the rep, whose tactful teaching gained her a powerful promoter.

Finally, don't be shy about your successes. Alert potential sponsors to your valuable assets. Since it can be difficult to toot your own horn, work with peers to sing each other's praises. A VP at Merrill Lynch described

(continued)

WHAT DO *YOU* BRING TO THE TABLE?

(*continued*)

how she and three other women, all high-potential leaders in different divisions of the firm, would meet monthly for lunch to update each other on their projects and accomplishments. The idea was to be ready to talk each other up, should an occasion arise. "So if my boss were to complain about some problem he's struggling to solve, I could say, 'You know, you should talk to Lisa in global equities, because she's had a lot of experience with that,'" this VP explained. "It turned out to be a really effective tactic, because we could be quite compelling about each other's accomplishments." In short order, all four women acquired sponsors and were promoted.

Adapted from "Make Yourself Sponsor-Worthy" by Sylvia Ann Hewlett on hbr.org, February 6, 2014 (product #H00NIB)

---

for sponsorship from collaborative, inclusive leaders because that style of leadership is one they embody or hope to emulate.

The problem is, those aren't the leaders with the power to push promising women to corporate heights. CTI research found that only 28% of men and women at U.S. companies say that inclusive collaborators represent the dominant style of leadership at their firm. Instead, nearly half of respondents—45%—say the most prevalent model is the classic, command-and-control leader who wants his lieutenants to fall in line behind him.

Twenty percent perceive their top management to be competitive types: hard-edged, hard-driving guys who value quarterly bottom-line results above all. Very few—only 6%—describe their chief as a charismatic visionary who, because he or she is focused on the big picture, seeks out tactical, pragmatic support.

In short, what female talent values and seeks in a sponsor just isn't on offer among those with real power in the organization. This profound mismatch helps explain why 40% of women fail to find the real deal: a sponsor who can deliver. As one woman ruefully told me, "I wasted 10 years talking to the wrong people."

To avoid that mistake, take the following advice.

- **Be strategic in your search.** Efficacy trumps affinity; you're looking not for a friend but an ally. Your targeted sponsor may exercise authority in a way you don't care to copy but it's their clout, not their style, that will turbocharge your career. Their powerful arsenal includes the high-level contacts they can introduce you to, the stretch assignments that will advance your career, their broad perspective when they give critical feedback—all ready to be deployed on behalf of their protégés.

- **Look beyond your immediate circle of mentors and managers.** While you should, of course, impress your boss—who can be a valuable connection to potential sponsors—seek out someone with real power to change your career. Would-be sponsors in large organizations are ideally two levels above you with line of sight to your role. In smaller firms, they're either the founder or president or are part of his or her inner circle.

Sponsors don't just magically appear, like fairy godmothers (or godfathers), to hardworking Cinderellas. Sponsorship must be earned—not once but continually. But when you link up to the right sponsor, the result can change your career.

———————

Sylvia Ann Hewlett is the founder and CEO of the Center for Talent Innovation and author of *Forget a Mentor, Find a Sponsor* (Harvard Business Review Press, 2013) and the forthcoming book, *The Sponsor Effect* (Harvard Business Review Press, 2019).

CHAPTER 11

Break Out of the Girls' Club

by Whitney Johnson

"There's a woman you *have* to meet," a male CEO said to me during a recent meeting.

"She sounds terrific," I responded. "I love meeting interesting people. Any men you'd like me to meet?"

"Aren't you married?"

"Sure am," I said. "Happily."

We both chuckled.

I then clarified, "In my experience, men have more power than women."

He agreed. "It's not a level playing field."

"Ergo, if a man with 500 people in his network, likely skewing male, only connects me with women he knows,

---

Adapted from "Are You Stuck in a Girls' Club?" on hbr.org, December 27, 2011 (product #H0085N)

then my power, or ability to get things done, is diminished," I explained.

As blogger Harris O'Malley writes in his online piece "Nerds and Male Privilege," "The reason why male privilege is so insidious is because of the insistence that it doesn't exist in the first place. That willful ignorance is key in keeping it in place; by pretending that the issue doesn't exist, it is that much easier to ensure that nothing ever changes."[1]

I will confess to thinking that women's professional inroads sometimes seem vexingly hard won, if won at all. There are clearly still major systemic changes that need to occur for women to achieve parity. But even stuck in our current reality you can do some things to advance your own career.

Seek Out Connections to Both Women and Men

In my experience, women tend to look to other women to make connections for them. We may feel more comfortable proceeding that way, but in order to gain enough power to make real progress, we have to seek out male help as collaborators, mentors, and connectors. The empirical evidence is undeniable that men can offer women power and a leg up in many ways that other women cannot. We need to leverage that reality.

If, as in my story above, the men you work with are offering you introductions to women but not men, remember that human beings look for patterns. In male-dominated fields, women CEOs are an anomaly. It's not surprising if men, seeing only two women in the room, assume that the women have something in common. Tara Hunt, CEO of Buyosphere, recalls one such introduction. A male venture capitalist said, "You two have to meet." Once on the phone with his referral, after several minutes of trying to find points of mutual interest, they finally ended up bonding over the guy who introduced them: "Do you think he introduced us because we are the only two women tech CEOs he knows?" "That's what I'm thinking." Hunt has now learned to ask for potential introductions (male or female) that can help move her business forward—and you should too.

Prepare for the Ask

Another male CEO who I had asked for potential contacts immediately rejoined, "I'd be happy to make introductions. Who do you want to meet?" For a minute I had no idea what to say. I recovered by asking for the option of a future introduction. I'm learning, though. Now when someone asks, I'll respond with something like: "Two things I'm trying to get done right now are to identify qualified purchasers for our fund and to get the word out about my book. Any introductions you could make along those lines would be welcome." Don't be afraid to be specific in your ask.

If it feels uncomfortable to be so bold, remember: The offer of an introduction is a compliment. There is always some reputational risk when we make an introduction. If one of your colleagues says, unprompted, "There's a person I want you to meet," that means the colleague is impressed with you and is signaling a willingness to use some portion of his political capital on your behalf.

93

Honor and Reciprocate Introductions Made by Women in Your Network

Given the relative value of introductions, women too may be inclined to make the really plum connections for and to men. Some years ago, I had made several key introductions on behalf of a young woman. When she decided to bring business to the firm, she bypassed me and went straight to my male colleagues. If a woman makes an introduction on your behalf, honor it. Madeleine Albright once said, "There's a special place in hell for women who don't help other women." In my opinion, there's a special place in hell for women who don't honor the hand extended to them by other women.

In academic circles and popular press, we read of breaking through the glass ceiling. But breaking through a ceiling implies a "storm the citadel" approach, requiring major changes to a system that may not be willing to acknowledge that a problem even exists. As the theory of disruptive innovation explains, the odds of success are low when we make a frontal assault on the status quo. But when we play on the periphery, opening one mind at a time, the odds go up that we'll push down our glass walls. Tear down those walls, and the ceiling just may come tumbling down.

Whitney Johnson is an executive coach, speaker, and innovation thinker. She was recently named one of the most influential management thinkers by Thinkers50. She is the author of *Build an A-Team* and the critically acclaimed *Disrupt Yourself.* Follow her on Twitter @johnsonwhitney.

NOTE

1. Harris O'Malley, "Nerds and Male Privilege," *Kotaku*, kotaku .com, December 16, 2011, https://kotaku.com/5868595/nerds -and-male-privilege.

CHAPTER 12

Make Yourself Safe for Sponsorship

by Sylvia Ann Hewlett

We can't avoid it: If you align yourself with a sponsor, people are going to notice, and they're going to talk. And some of that talk is going to insinuate that your relationship is sexual. Women, particularly young women, have it worst of all on this front.

According to my research, 95% of men and 93% of women say they find it easiest to give and receive guidance in a one-on-one setting. Yet 64% of men in senior positions (vice president and higher) and 50% of up-and-coming women admit they're hesitant to initiate any sort of one-on-one interaction with a coworker of the opposite gender lest their motives be misconstrued

Adapted from content posted on hbr.org, October 7, 2013

by their colleagues and rumors start poisoning the workplace. This may come as a shock to the many men and women who thought they left that sort of gossip behind in high school, but unfortunately, it still exists. And it hurts ambitious women's chances for promotion.

Consider the example of a woman we'll call Jana. Soon after being promoted to vice president at a major financial services firm, Jana became aware that her boss was holding regular meetings with the four other VPs (all men) at his home over barbecued ribs and beer. "He invited them but excluded me," she said, "and then they'd all lie to me at work about where they'd been that weekend." Months went by. Finally, she was issued an invitation—and immediately spotted the problem. "Here I was, a youngish woman out on the pool deck with the guys, with my boss's wife hovering in the kitchen, peering out at us."

Jana could see how difficult it was for her boss to include her in any informal work gathering outside the office. But by excluding her, he signaled to the rest of the management team that she was not part of the inner circle. She knew full well, too, that the men had developed a special camaraderie by meeting outside of work and that she had lost out on the trust built up over months.

Today, Jana is a managing director, two reports away from the CEO, but she feels her rate of progression suffered because she had no sponsors. The reason for her lack of sponsorship? She couldn't figure out how to mitigate the risk of career-wrecking rumors for her male superiors. "There were men I reported to who wouldn't get into a cab with me, who wouldn't allow their admin to schedule them on the same flight," she recalled. "Looking back, I think this is what kept me always just outside the inner circle. I had a couple of near misses with sponsorship, but in the end, my bosses just couldn't afford to go there with me."

Sexual tension in the workplace is a problem that's not going to go away—ever. But whether a possible sexual relationship with a superior is real or imagined, it's the fastest way to sabotage sponsorship. That presents a tough conundrum. How do you make yourself safe for sponsorship?

There are ways you can ensure that your relationship with your sponsor appears professional and nothing more. Consider the following tips.

- **Always telegraph professionalism.** Take notice of your appearance. Look polished but not provocative. Seventy-three percent of leaders surveyed for the Center for Talent Innovation's research on executive presence cite provocative clothing as the number one appearance blunder for a woman attempting to climb the career ladder. This is not to suggest that you have to lose your personal style in the workplace. But it's imperative that your clothing, makeup, hairstyle, body language, and communication style don't give the wrong impression.

- **Meet your sponsor in public.** Bagels and coffee in the conference room, lunch on campus, or a restaurant well-trafficked by office personnel where you can take the opportunity to wave to colleagues and demonstrate that you have nothing to hide—

these are safe choices. Dinner on a business trip may be unavoidable, but make sure the venue isn't the kind of place you'd ever go on a date. Ideally, you'll want to make meeting with your sponsor a routine, choosing the same time and place in each case. Consistency ensures that nothing will appear irregular about meeting your sponsor one-on-one.

- **Don't hide your private life.** Talk about your significant others—your spouse, partner, kids—and introduce them to your sponsor. Publicize your outside commitments to your church or temple, athletic league, or community organization. If you're comfortable, put photos on your desk or screensaver that assure others you have a network of emotional ties outside of work. By doing so, you'll telegraph the completeness of your private life and minimize the possibility that others will perceive an ulterior agenda.

- **Silence gossip by proving that you're special.** When people complain that you're receiving special attention, they're insinuating that you don't deserve it. Acting surprised or overly nice only reinforces their belief that you've got something to hide. Squelch those rumors by wowing everyone with the quality of your work, the extra hours you're putting in, and the special skills you're contributing. In a word, *own* your special status, and demonstrate why you deserve it.

Sponsorship is vital to fulfilling your potential, turbo-charging your career, and delivering your dreams. During economic downturns and corporate restructuring, it's often the only thing between you and the door. So strengthen your career springboard—and your safety net—by finding a sponsor and signaling your professional relationship.

———————

Sylvia Ann Hewlett is the founder and CEO of the Center for Talent Innovation and author of *Forget a Mentor, Find a Sponsor* (Harvard Business Review Press, 2013) and the forthcoming book, *The Sponsor Effect* (Harvard Business Review Press, 2019).

Position Yourself for Leadership

CHAPTER 13

"Feminine" Values Can Give Leaders an Edge

by John Gerzema

The 2013 Pew Center study, "Breadwinner Moms," revealed that working mothers are the sole or primary provider in a record 40% of U.S. households. Only a few days before the report was released, hedge fund billionaire Paul Tudor-Jones created a stir by remarking at a conference that women will never rival men as traders because babies are a "focus killer."

Here we have the dynamics of a new economy colliding with the old establishment like tectonic plates. But

Adapted from "'Feminine' Values Can Give Tomorrow's Leaders an Edge" on hbr.org, August 12, 2013 as developed nations restructure from manufacturing to knowledge and services, my bet is on the moms—or more specifically, the women—and the men who can think like them. Survey data my colleague Michael D'Antonio and I gathered from 64,000 people in nationally representative samples in 13 countries, from the Americas and Europe to Asia, point to widespread dissatisfaction with typically "male" ways of doing business and a growing appreciation for the traits, skills, and competencies that are perceived as more feminine.

The results, published in our book *The Athena Doctrine*, reveal that 57% of people were dissatisfied with the conduct of men in their country, including 79% of Japanese and South Koreans and more than two-thirds of people in Indonesia, Mexico, the United Kingdom, and the United States. This sentiment is amplified among the millennial generation of whom nearly 80% are dissatisfied—most notably in highly masculine societies like Brazil, South Korea, Japan, and India.

If people have grown cold on male-dominated structures and leadership, they also offer a solution: Two-thirds of survey respondents felt that "The world would be a better place if men thought more like women," including 76% in France and Brazil and 70% in Germany. Those stats include majorities of men who equate masculine incumbency with income disparity, continuing high levels of unemployment, and political gridlock.

Curious as to how leaders could "think more like women," we asked half our sample—32,000 people around the world—to classify 125 human characteristics as either masculine, feminine, or neither, while the other half were asked to rate the same words (without assigning them to a gender on their importance to leadership, success, morality, and happiness. Statistical modeling revealed strong consensus that what people felt was "feminine" they also deemed essential to leading in an increasingly social, interdependent, and transparent world. (See table 13-1.)

We next visited 18 countries, where we interviewed more than 100 innovative women and men in medicine, politics, education, startups, NGOs, and other sectors of the economy. Here are two of many examples we came across that show how anyone can lead with a more feminine ethos.

TABLE 13-1

Top 10 competencies desired for modern leaders

Here are the most highly correlated characteristics for the "ideal modern leader" based on a survey of 64,000 people around the world.

Viewed as feminine	Viewed as masculine
1. Expressive	
2. Plans for future	
	3. Decisive
4. Reasonable	
5. Loyal	
6. Flexible	
7. Patient	
	8. Resilient
9. Intuitive	
10. Collaborative	

Source: John Gerzema, BAV Consulting, WPP Group plc, 2012.

Empathy Is Innovation

While leaders spend considerable time and effort trying to envision markets and push out innovation, empathy can often generate simple yet breakthrough ideas. In her years working as an advocate for charities in Britain and in other countries, Anna Pearson noticed a pattern: There were many people who wanted to volunteer but were too busy (or had schedules that were too varied) to commit to a cause. To bridge the gap between what volunteers could give and what people needed, Anna reimagined volunteering on a very small scale. Her London-based nonprofit Spots of Time connects organizations with people who can give an hour or so at a time and often at a moment's notice. The lesson? Anna trained her empathy not just on beneficiaries of charity but also on volunteers. That kindness and sensitivity to others was the catalyst for creativity.

Vulnerability Is Strength

You can't read a business article today without encountering learning from failure. But maybe there would be less failing if we were willing to admit what we don't know in the first place. In Berlin we met Ijad Madisch, a Harvard-trained virologist who kept "getting stuck" in his experiments. When he asked his colleagues for help, he was chastised. Big-time scientists were supposed to project an image of supreme competence. Madisch realized that science needed a global community where the work took precedence over egos. So he started ResearchGate, a social network for scientists, which now has some 3 million members across 200 countries. By letting down his guard and showing candor and humility, Madisch not only helped himself but also inspired others to join his cause. This advanced research far more rapidly than the old approach of working in cubicles and meeting at conferences.

Today's work requires a new leadership paradigm. If you want to be successful, look at the list of competencies outlined here and—whether you're a man or a woman—start working on them.

John Gerzema is CEO of The Harris Poll and a fellow at the Athena Center for Leadership Studies at Barnard College. He is a coauthor of the book *The Athena Doctrine: How Women (and the Men Who Think Like Them) Will Rule the Future,* the proceeds of which support the United Nations Foundation's Girl Up Campaign.

CHAPTER 14

The Upside and Downside of Collaborative Leadership

by Jill Flynn, Kathryn Heath, and Mary Davis Holt

A few years ago we hosted a seminar for 150 business-women. The topic for the morning was "Power: Do Women Really Want It?" Just imagine the noise level when that many smart and engaged female managers debated the pros and cons of wielding power. As the session came to a close, we asked for a tally of how the

Adapted from "Collaboration's Hidden Tax on Women's Careers" on hbr.org, November 11, 2011

breakout groups had answered the question. Their response was unanimous yet equivocal. Do women really want power? "Yes and no."

Many of these women already held senior leadership positions in large companies. The others were in the room because they had been identified by their organizations as high potentials. Still, they could not fully come to terms with their ambition. One of the big reasons these women cited for their wishy-washy perspective? They strongly preferred to collaborate and cooperate rather than brazenly call the shots.

In our coaching sessions, we've worked with countless women who are exceptionally collaborative leaders. They have a talent for establishing buy-in. Still, the art of consensus can sometimes slow women down and diminish their leadership credibility. Over the past decade, we've interviewed more than 1,700 people to find out how women can be more successful at the highest levels in leadership. One thing we've heard again and again is that collaboration can be a double-edged sword in terms of being perceived as powerful.

It's easy to make the case that collaborative leadership is the wave of the future: Technology makes decentralized decision making and flat organizations more feasible than ever. The problem is that an overemphasis on consensus can be viewed as weak. We've seen collaboration go wrong for women when they do the following three things:

Ask for permission

We teach children to ask for permission, but when that behavior occurs with regularity as an adult it is seen as overly deferential. Asking permission can be perceived as avoiding responsibility or an unwillingness to make tough decisions. Even beyond the negative perception it creates, a need for approval means you can't act as quickly as other colleagues who are confident enough to proceed without hesitation. Leaders need to be willing to take risks and make difficult decisions independently.

Appear indecisive

There are plenty of instances when a decision requires careful consideration, conversation, and analysis. However, there are also many other times when you need to give yourself the green light to proceed. Making the tough calls on your own and getting closure quickly means you need to be comfortable delivering bad news or taking the opposing position. It's acceptable to be the dissenter or to play the devil's advocate as long as you have the ammunition to make a good case. If you can do so in a firm, non-emotional way, people will respect you for your decisiveness and expediency.

Fail to assert a strong point of view

Countless times we've seen well-meaning managers dilute their authority by failing to emphasize their perspective or corral an important discussion. Collaboration gone bad can mean your executive oversight and guiding perspective gets drowned out in the din. Suddenly, decisions are being made by committee. If you are not setting a clear agenda, considerable time and resources may be wasted in meetings and initiatives that are circuitous. The best collaborative leaders are able to maintain their executive presence: They articulate a vision, provide inspiration, and then give their teams enough latitude to creatively and effectively work toward a defined end that suits the organization.

Being a collaborative leader can be a tremendous asset when used judiciously. Women who can retain this core ability, while at the same time acting decisively to make things happen, will have the skills and demeanor to thrive.

―――――――――

Jill Flynn is a partner at Flynn Heath Holt Leadership, which specializes in leadership development programs and executive coaching for women. She is a coauthor of *Break Your Own Rules: How to Change the Patterns of Thinking That Block Women's Paths to Power*. **Kathryn Heath** is a partner at Flynn Heath Holt Leadership. She is a coauthor of *The Influence Effect: A New Path to Power for Women*. **Mary Davis Holt, MBA,** is a senior consultant with Flynn Heath Holt Leadership, and she is a coauthor of *Break Your Own Rules: How to Change the Patterns of Thinking That Block Women's Paths to Power*. Follow them on Twitter @FlynnHeathHolt.

CHAPTER 15

Women and the Vision Thing

*A summary of the full-length HBR article "Women and the Vision Thing" by **Herminia Ibarra** and **Otilia Obodaru**, highlighting key ideas and advice for developing your visioning skills.*

IDEA IN BRIEF

Women are still a minority in the top ranks of business. The reason? Their perceived lack of vision, according to Ibarra and Obodaru. In 360-degree feedback, women score relatively low on key elements of visioning, including ability to sense opportunities and threats, to set strategic direction, and to inspire constituents.

Excerpted from "Women and the Vision Thing," *Harvard Business Review*, January 2009 (product #R0901E)

The authors' research suggests three explanations for women's low visioning scores:

- Some women don't buy into the value of being visionary.

- Some women lack the confidence to go out on a limb with an untested vision.

- Some women who develop a vision in collaboration with their teams don't get credit for having created one.

Regardless of the cause, women seeking more senior roles must be perceived as visionary leaders. They can start by understanding what "being visionary" means in practical terms—and then honing their visioning skills.

IDEA IN PRACTICE

What "Being Visionary" Means

Being visionary is a matter of exercising three skills well, as seen in table 15-1.

How to Strengthen Your Visioning Skills

- **Appreciate the importance of visioning.** Recognize vision as a matter of not just style but substance. It's not about meaningless vision statements but about strategic acumen and positioning your know-how.

TABLE 15-1

Skill	How to exercise it
Sensing opportunities and threats in the environment	• Simplify complex situations by identifying broad-stroke patterns. • Foresee events that will affect your organization. • Conduct a vigorous exchange with an array of people inside and outside the organization.
Setting strategic direction	• Encourage new business. • Generate ideas for new strategies. • Make decisions with an eye toward the big picture.
Inspiring constituents	• Frame current practices as inadequate. • Be open to new ways of doing things. • Encourage others to look beyond limitations. • Communicate new and better possibilities in clear, compelling ways.

- **Leverage (or build) your network.** Formulating a vision demands a solid grasp of what's happening outside your group and organization. A good external network is the first line of defense against the insular thinking that can hurt your visioning ability.

- **Learn the craft.** Much of visioning can be learned the old-fashioned way: at the elbow of a master. Find role models and study how they develop and communicate strategic ideas. Then work with a coach to identify training and tools to build your capabilities.

- **Let go of old roles.** When you're very good at a needed task, the whole organization will conspire to keep you at it. For instance, even if delivering on the details has always been your ticket to advancement, it won't help you with visioning. Resist the urge to stay in the weeds.

- **Constantly communicate.** As you develop a vision, find opportunities to articulate it. Don't wait until it's perfect. Try out draft versions along the way, even after the vision has come into sharp focus. You won't be seen as a visionary unless you get the word out.

- **Step up to the plate.** A vision comes not only from the outside but also from greater self-confidence. Believe in your ability and assume responsibility for creating a new and better future for others in your organization.

Herminia Ibarra is the Charles Handy Professor of Organizational Behavior at London Business School. Prior to joining LBS, she served on the INSEAD and Harvard Business School faculties. An authority on leadership and career development, Ibarra is ranked among the most influential management thinkers in the world by Thinkers50. Her most recent book, *Act Like a Leader, Think Like a Leader* (Harvard Business Review Press, 2015), explains how to step up to a bigger leadership role. She received her PhD from Yale University, where she was a National Science Fellow. **Otilia Obodaru** is a PhD student in organizational behavior at INSEAD.

CHAPTER 16

Finding Your True Self at Work

An interview with Tina Opie

Editor's note: Tina Opie was interviewed by HBR editors Amy Bernstein, Sarah Green Carmichael, and Nicole Torres.

Authenticity is what it feels like when you can bring your whole self to work—when your behavior matches your intentions. Researchers have found that feeling authentic at the office has been linked to higher engagement, more workplace satisfaction, improved performance and better overall well-being. That's why authentic

---

Adapted from "Lead with Authenticity" on *Women at Work* (HBR podcast), February 9, 2018

leadership has become something of a gold standard at many companies today.

But there's a challenge for women who want to be authentic at work. There are expectations about how we should look or communicate—and that's especially difficult for women of color. How can do you strike the right balance of representing your true self while conforming to company standards?

In this interview, we talk with Tina Opie, an assistant professor of management at Babson College, who studies authentic leadership.

HBR: I worked with a woman once who was pulled aside by our boss and told, "You know, you have a lot of potential. I can see you moving into management. But if you want to do that, you need to dress differently, and you should start wearing makeup." Everyone in this case was a woman, but my peer who'd been given this advice was furious: "That is so sexist. I can't believe she would say that I have to wear makeup to get ahead in this company." Is it sexist to give someone that kind of advice?

Tina Opie: We have to differentiate between how we want the world to be and how the world actually is. I'd love it if that advice never had to be heard or uttered because if this is the way you want to go to work, you should be completely fine as long as you're doing an amazing job. That's the kind of world I want to live in, and that's the kind of world that I've dedicated my research and teaching toward building. But unfortunately, that is not the world we live in. We live in a world where impressions matter and where appearance is highly connected to impressions.

You all have done a lot of research here at HBR on the way that humans automatically categorize other people. It's instantaneous. And because of those types of connections, we automatically think, "OK. This kind of person is going to be more professional; that kind of person is not going to be professional." If you happen to fall into the latter category, you may have to do some additional work to demonstrate that you are in fact fierce, professional, and amazing. But that may come after the fact, after that initial impression that you are not those things.

I graduated from college with a wardrobe that consisted of two pairs of blue jeans and three button-down shirts. My mother, who was an advertising executive, took me shopping before I started my first job. She made me buy a straight skirt, a nice jacket, and a nice blouse. I could not have felt more uncomfortable and less authentic. And her advice to me was if you want to be the vice president eventually, dress like the vice president. All these years later, I still think about it because that was excellent advice to someone who didn't understand what being authentic in the new context would be. What do you think of that?

What your mother did was provide you with a uniform. We don't like to think of ourselves as professionals having to wear uniforms. It's a little bit classist. In our minds, we're above that, we're more professional. That's for other people, to have to have to wear uniforms.

But the business suit is, in fact, a uniform. I have done some research about the origins of the business suit, which is very Eurocentric. It comes from royal court; it was very masculine. It was actually created as a way to differentiate the classes from one another and to show a certain level of modesty. Because initially, while the suits were super brilliant in color—reds, purples, and so on—eventually they had toned down to what we now have—navies, blacks, grays, very subdued subtle colors—because that conveyed and communicated a certain level of professionalism and trustworthiness.

Your mother was extending to you the same kind of advice. By suggesting you wear a uniform, she was introducing you to—or hoping to socialize you into—a new world. The corporate world was new for you; you had no idea. If you had shown up with those jeans and one of those button-down shirts, you probably would've been flabbergasted and embarrassed when you got there because no one else would've been attired in that way.

Now, I will also say that right now I have on jeggings, a nice floral top, some cute earrings, and my hair is up in a puff. I hope to run a corporation where I can be the CEO and be dressed exactly this way. And I dare anybody to come in there and tell me I'm unprofessional. But I also want to have a corporation where if someone is more comfortable in a business suit, they feel comfortable wearing that.

What is a conversation like with your students, when someone is asking for advice about how to dress for the job interview? How to wear her hair and such?

I have a former student who has now graduated from Babson named Nadia. I was doing a workshop on authenticity in the workplace at Babson, and she said, "I see that you wear your hair natural. Do you think it's OK if I wear my hair natural in the workplace?" I walked her through the decision. I said, "Listen, do you like your natural hair?" "Yes, I feel good about it," she said. "It makes me feel good as a black, Latina woman. That's really what I'd like to do." Great. We're establishing the fact that that is connected to her authenticity and her identity.

Then I said, "Where are you interested in going?" "I want to go into law." OK. So Nadia, describe for me the kind of context or environment you think you're going to confront in the legal profession. "Well, they're very conservative and wear tailored suits." And when she said "they," she was describing men. We quickly discussed the women in that environment, and it was very similar. I don't think we can escape the fact that initially, women's business attire was very much created to replicate or duplicate men's business attire. Women's uniforms in the workplace were designed to cover up their femininity and their differences.

So the first thing I established with Nadia was what her authentic identity was. Then we established the legal context. And here comes the difficult part. People would like there to be a clear-cut answer, but there is not. I told her that she has to weigh the consequences. If your hair is authentic to you, or if you feel like you're giving up, you're selling yourself out, or you're conforming to a point where it just makes you uncomfortable, then perhaps that's not the best decision. But understand that if you walk into this particular context, it may mean that you don't get the job interview. You don't get the job, or you don't get the assignments.

The alternative is that you conform and you straighten your hair. For many people of African descent, when we say conform, what we mean when it comes to their hair is to cover it, to straighten it, to get rid of any visible evidence of your Africanness, of your blackness. You can do that, but if that is going to make you feel bad about yourself, then maybe that's not the best place for you to be. Now, that is a very privileged comment to make, because if you have to pay your bills, you're straightening your hair. You're going to cover up the tattoo, you're going to get rid of the piercings, you're going to do what it takes.

Now, there are some people that might say well, we would like her more if she was a little whiter. I can't do anything with my skin color. I guess I can, but I'm not willing to. The cost of that is so high that most people are not willing to do that. But we do have instances of people who are willing to change their names, right? We've seen that quite a bit, specifically in the Asian community. I have many students who will say "Just call me Amy." I want to call them by the name that's on their birth certificate, but for them that is uncomfortable because it calls out their Asianness. What I want to get to is a place in the workforce where we are all able to bring who we authentically identify as and describe ourselves to be in the workforce—and our colleagues and classmates embrace that, rather than trying to get us to conform.

Aside from appearance, how else do we think about authenticity in the workplace?

It could be the way that you communicate. I was once told that I was too ethnic because I speak with my hands. But what was interesting is the clients loved me. They thought I was such a great storyteller. So the way that you communicate, your accent, the way that you even articulate anger, disagreement, or conflict—some people will avoid it at all costs. Other people will dive right in.

How is communicating different from how you dress? For instance, some women are prone to up-speak, where women end their sentences in the form of a question. How is getting rid of these vocal habits different from dressing differently to conform?

Well, see that's the question. I don't know. Because we're trying to figure the boundary lines, right? We're trying to figure out how can this person be authentic and excel in the workplace.

I'm from the south. I do not have much of a southern accent unless I'm angry or if I'm really tired. And that is because my parents raised us to not have a southern accent because they recognized that that might be inhibiting to our academic as well as career success. Should I have done that? Would I be more authentic if I still had my southern accent, given that I was raised by two people from the south? I don't know. I was willing to give that up. I'm not willing to relax my hair though. That's the line for me. So for some people who are speaking when they have that lilt at the end, most of the time it's unconscious, which is why I would say it might not be so connected to their authenticity. They're not even aware that they're doing that. It's a bad habit, as opposed to a critical component of their authentic identity.

I also wonder how much of it is generational—the way I think vocal fry is generational. How much of it is about conformity to generational norms?

Some of it is. And I've had to check myself because there was someone who I thought, I don't enjoy the way he speaks. He's an amazing entrepreneur. Then I paused and said, Why am I trying to get him to speak proper English? He's communicating, he's passionate, he's articulate, he's brilliant. Why do I need him to not have that kind of accent?

Yeah. I've found myself in conversations being too distracted by the fry or the up-speak to pay attention. But then I have to remind myself to listen to the substance. It takes a certain amount of discipline.

Is that because we stereotype people who speak with this deeper, gravelly voice—the fry, as we call it? We stereotype them as lazy, incompetent? I think we have to unpack that when we have an interaction. And I would say for women who are at work, for women who are supervising other women, for men who are supervising women, when you're across from someone and you're finding yourself being distracted by something—the Afro, the hand gestures, the fry and the voice, the cleavage, the lipstick or the lack thereof, the hairstyle—ask yourself what is really happening? Is it because this person is not comporting with your ideal of a professional?

How are authenticity and the expectations of authenticity different for women of different races?

I have done some research with Katherine Phillips of Columbia Business School on hair in the workplace— hair penalties in particular. The reason I studied hair is because it's a mutable trait that you can alter and it's very relevant to identity. As a black woman in corporate America, I had been advised not to wear my hair in particular styles because the clients might not like it. When we conducted our experimental research, we found that Afrocentric hair, meaning textured hair—and not all women of African descent have the same textured hair—but people with Afros or dreadlocks in their hair were rated as less professional than the same images of women when they were portrayed as having straight relaxed hair. And that was across the board, by black and white people.

What was interesting was that we found that while Afrocentric hair was denigrated across the board, it was most denigrated by people of African descent. There was an in-group bias that we found. And we still have to do follow-up research to examine that, because some people immediately said that's because black people hate themselves. I was, like, OK. I don't hate myself. That's not necessarily the case. There could be some kind of internalized racism, but it could also be that black people are keenly aware of the impression management techniques that are necessary to successfully navigate the workplace. So when we asked questions like, "What advice would you give to this candidate?" they didn't mention hair at all to the people with straight hair. But when black people in particular were seeing these black images with Afros or dreadlocks, they would say things like, "She might need to change her hairstyle"; "she might need to straighten her hair"; "she might need to relax her hair." And I think the reason they were emphasizing that is because it's probably advice that they received both inside and outside of the workplace.

People have no idea how much time it takes to groom your hair if it is naturally textured and every day you're having to figure out how to make it straight. That's a lot of shadow work, a lot of uncompensated work that you're doing outside of the workplace. There's a lot of thinking that goes into how to do this. Wouldn't we rather have employees who are focused on their work? And this is not to say that people of African descent are distracted at work. It's just that they're having to put in extra for the same thing. And really, is it even related to the work? What does it have to do with the job? It is simply a cultural understanding of what is and is not professional. And that's what I want the takeaway to be, that organizations really and truly need to check themselves. There have been lawsuits where people have been hired and then had job offers reneged upon because they wouldn't cut off their dreadlocks. I mean really, what are we even talking about? You're telling me that as an organization, you're so concerned that your clientele is going to be offended by this hairstyle that you would fire someone that you thought was highly qualified to perform this role? Now, maybe we have rules like you need to be clean. But even that, believe it or not, can be debatable in terms of what is clean and what is not. We really need to wrestle with our cultural understanding of what is professional.

Do you think it's possible for a woman to be a truly authentic leader?

I do think it's possible for women to be authentic leaders, and that means a person who is expressing herself, who has reflected on the kind of person and the values that she wants to bring to the workplace and who is willing to offer that and share that, pros and cons, with the people who are following her.

Now, what I'm struggling with is authentic *leadership*. The definition of the term can shift depending on what you're talking about. Do we mean someone who's honest and transparent? Or do we mean someone who is pursuing their best self? I mean someone who is pursuing their best self, who is working to take the perspectives of the people who follow them so that they can take that into consideration when they're making decisions. I mean someone who, if I decide to wear my Afro, I'm going to bring all of that to the table.

Yes, I think it's possible for women to be authentic and to be leaders in that way. I do not think it's necessarily limited to certain kinds of women, but I do think it's harder for women. The less power you have, the more challenging it can be to be authentic, period. If you're a person who is an hourly worker who is really dependent upon their employer, if your boss tells you to wear an apron and straighten your hair, you may be more inclined to do that than if you are the CEO of an organization. We have to be sensitive to the fact that it's not as easy for everyone. And I think power, again, rears its head and impacts women's and men's ability to be authentic in the workplace and to be authentic leaders.

Tina Opie is an assistant professor in the management division at Babson College, teaching organizational behavior courses to undergraduates and MBA students. Her research focuses on how organizations and individuals can cocreate workplaces that successfully leverage individual difference, convey respect for individuals' unique identities and contributions, and encourage authenticity in the workplace. She is also the founder of hairasidentity.com and naturalhairatwork.com.

Negotiate for What You Want

CHAPTER 17

Why Women Don't Negotiate Their Job Offers

by Hannah Riley Bowles

Research shows that women are more hesitant than men to negotiate their salary offers. For instance, one study of graduating MBA students found that half of the men had negotiated their job offers as compared to only one-eighth of the women.[1] This general pattern has been replicated in survey studies of working adults and in laboratory experiments.[2] It begs the question: Why? Is this a confidence problem? Is negotiation a skill for which men are simply better socialized than women? Why leave money on the table?

Adapted from content posted on hbr.org, June 19, 2014

Researchers have examined the why, and the answer has more to do with how women are treated when they negotiate than it has to do with their general confidence or skills at negotiation.[3] Numerous studies have been conducted in which participants rate their impressions of employees who negotiate for pay and of employees who let the same opportunity to negotiate pass. The researchers then compared people's willingness to work with that employee after evaluators saw him or her negotiate. If evaluators were less inclined to work with the same employee after seeing him or her negotiate, that suggests the employee paid a "social cost" for negotiating for higher pay.

In repeated studies, the social cost of negotiating for higher pay has been found to be greater for women than it is for men. Men can certainly overplay their hand and alienate negotiating counterparts. However, in most published studies, the social cost of negotiating for pay is not significant for men, while it *is* significant for women.

The results of this research are important to understand before one criticizes a woman—or a woman criticizes herself—for being reluctant to negotiate for more pay. Women's reticence is based on an accurate read of the social environment. Women get a nervous feeling about negotiating for higher pay because they are intuiting—correctly—that self-advocating for higher pay would present a socially difficult situation for them, more so than for men.

But here's a twist: We love it when women negotiate assertively *for others*. It's just when women are negotiating assertively for *themselves*—particularly around pay—where we find a backlash. Unsurprisingly, research also shows that women perform better (negotiate higher salaries, for example) when their role is to advocate for others as opposed to negotiating for more for themselves.[4] Men's behavior and the ensuing social effects don't shift much depending on whether they are advocating for themselves or others.

So we shouldn't blame women for being more hesitant than men to negotiate for higher pay. But is there anything that women can do about it? Thankfully, yes.

The answer is to use a "relational account"—or what I have learned from Sheryl Sandberg of Facebook to call a "think personally, act communally" strategy. Using a relational account or "I-We" strategy involves asking for what you want while signaling to your negotiating counterpart that you are also taking their perspective. So how does it work?

First, you want to explain to your negotiating counterpart why—in *their* eyes—it's legitimate for you to be negotiating (in other words, appropriate or justified under the circumstances). In her book *Lean In: Women, Work, and the Will to Lead*, Sandberg describes her negotiations with Facebook, where she told them, "Of course you realize that you're hiring me to run your deal team, so you want me to be a good negotiator." She wanted Facebook to see her negotiating as legitimate because, if she didn't negotiate, they should be worried about whether they'd made the right hire.

Second, you want to signal to your negotiating counterpart that you care about organizational relationships.

After pointing out that they should want her to be a good negotiator, Sheryl recounts saying, "This is the only time you and I will ever be on opposite sides of the table." In other words, "I am clear that we're on the same team here."

In experimental research testing evaluators' impressions of alternative negotiating scripts, we found that relational accounts (these "I-We" strategies) helped women both get what they wanted *and* make the impression that they wanted to make. For instance, one successful relational account that we tested was very similar to Sheryl's, but was written for a more junior employee: "I don't know how typical it is for people at my level to negotiate, but I'm hopeful that you'll see my skill at negotiating as something important that I can bring to the job." Note that I'm not suggesting that women use these scripts word-for-word. Come up with an "I-We" strategy that makes sense in context and feels authentic to you.

When the explanation for why the woman was negotiating seemed legitimate, people were more inclined to grant her compensation request (as compared to when she was simply negotiating for a higher salary without that explanation). When her script communicated concern for organizational relationships, evaluators were more inclined to work with her. Indeed, there was no significant difference in the willingness to work with a female employee who negotiated using a relational account as compared to female employees who did not negotiate for a raise at all. Variation in the negotiation scripts did not significantly influence the evaluations of male negotiators.

I should highlight that not every legitimate explanation for negotiating helped women. For instance, conventional wisdom in the negotiation community has been to negotiate for a raise when you have another job offer. We tested multiple negotiation scripts based on an outside offer—even ones suggesting that the offer just dropped in the employee's lap. Unfortunately, in all of the outside-offer scripts we tested, the suggestion that the employee would leave if the offer were not matched seemed to undermine the impression that the employee cared about organizational relationships. As a result, evaluators reported being more willing to grant a woman with an outside offer a raise, but they were disinclined to work with her (as compared to if she let the opportunity to negotiate pass). The outside-offer scripts had no significant effects on the evaluation of male negotiators.

The key to an "I-We" strategy is to explain why your counterpart should perceive your negotiating as legitimate in terms that also communicate your concern for organizational relationships.

I should acknowledge that this idea of using relational accounts drives some women crazy. It makes them feel like they are bending to unjust stereotypes or simply being inauthentic. I sympathize with that reaction. We were surprised while doing the research that it would be so hard to make the backlash effects go away. But every movement needs its idealists and pragmatists, and I am playing the pragmatist here.

It is good advice for *any* negotiator—male or female— to ask for what they want in terms that their counterpart will perceive as legitimate and mutually beneficial.

But for women, it is especially helpful because it unburdens them from the social costs of self-advocating. By sharing this research, I hope to shed light on that bias. Most people don't want to discriminate. With more self-awareness as negotiators and evaluators of these biases and more women negotiating successfully for higher pay, we can close this gender gap.

———————

Hannah Riley Bowles is a senior lecturer and chair of the Management, Leadership, and Decision Sciences Area at the Harvard Kennedy School. She is the faculty director of Women & Power, the Kennedy School's executive program for women in senior leadership from the public, private, and nonprofit sectors, and a leading expert on how gender influences pay negotiations and negotiation as a micro-mechanism of inequality.

NOTES

1. Deborah A. Small et al., "Who Goes to the Bargaining Table? The Influence of Gender and Framing on the Initiation of Negotiation," *Journal of Personality and Social Psychology* 93, no. 4 (October 2007), 600–613.

2. Katharina G. Kugler et al., "Gender Differences in the Propensity to Initiate Negotiations: A Meta-Analysis," working paper no. 2013/3, Ludwig-Maximilians-Universiaet Muenchen, Munich, Germany, 2013, http://www.psy.lmu.de/wirtschaftspsychologie/forschung/working_papers/wop2013_3.pdf.

3. Hannah Riley Bowles, Linda Babcock, and Lei Lai, "Social Incentives for Gender Differences in the Propensity to Initiate Negotiations: Sometimes It Does Hurt to Ask," *Organizational Behavior and Human Decision Processes* 103, issue 1 (May 2007): 84–103.

4. Hannah Riley Bowles, Linda Babcock, and Kathleen L. McGinn, "Constraints and Triggers: Situational Mechanics of Gender in Negotiation," *Journal of Personality and Social Psychology* 89, no. 6 (December 2005): 951–965.

CHAPTER 18

Having the Here's-What-I-Want Conversation with Your Boss

by Rebecca Shambaugh

One person stands between you and your next raise or promotion: your boss. While others on the leadership team—and even your peers—may exert some influence on your career future, it's your direct supervisor who can pull the strings to either grant or deny your chance for advancement. But to get what you want, you have to ask for it.

Adapted from content posted on hbr.org, November 20, 2015 (product #H02IBL)

Despite this truth, research from the Society of Human Resource Management has found that nearly 80% of people feel uncomfortable discussing salary and other employment terms.

I spoke recently at a conference in New York, and a female executive pulled me aside to ask my advice on this topic. She explained that while she was on the verge of being promoted to the C-suite, her family situation with three children had many demands. She was feeling conflicted about whether or not she could take on higher-level responsibilities while remaining both a strong professional and strong parent. In confidence, she shared with me that she was planning to resign from her position and company later that month. I then asked her, "Did you consider going to your boss and asking directly for what you want—maybe some additional time off or even going part-time for a while—to facilitate your ability to accept the promotion while still making more time for family?" My point was that, whether it involves a promotion, a raise, or another goal, it doesn't have to be all or nothing when it comes to your career—*if* you learn how to identify what you want and then confidently ask for it.

At its core, the act of asking your superior for something important to your career progression may make you feel vulnerable. (See the sidebar "But What If They Say No?") But summoning the courage to do so actually demonstrates strength. Whether you seek more money, higher status, increased visibility, additional resources, or more time off, you likely won't get it if you don't specifically ask for it. What's more, when it comes

BUT WHAT IF THEY SAY NO?

by Judith White

Fear of being turned down stems from a natural concern that you'll feel ashamed and upset if your proposal is rejected. My colleagues and I have found that feeling this way is most likely when your proposal is personal: when what you ask for reflects your personal value or worth. Fear of losing face is a powerful motivator for avoiding a negotiation. In fact, the more you believe you deserve what you ask for, the more you risk losing face if your request is denied.

To overcome this fear, try to reframe the negotiation. Stop thinking about how bad you'll feel if you hear no. Think instead about how good you'll feel when you've initiated the conversation. Then you'll be *saving* face if you have the discussion and *losing* face if you continue to avoid it. In her book *Knowing Your Value*, Mika Brzezinski shares her journey of reframing her salary negotiation. Remember, your self-worth does not depend on what *they* say; it depends on what *you* say and how you present yourself.

Judith White is a visiting associate professor of management at the Tuck School of Business at Dartmouth.

Adapted from "Overcome Your Reluctance and Start Negotiating Your Salary" on hbr.org, May 19, 2016 (product #H02WAT)

to achieving the next step up in pay, position, or prefer-ences, many bosses *expect* you to ask for what you want directly. Asking shows both self-confidence and respect for your boss by acknowledging that you're requesting, not just expecting, help.

Assuming that you've already done your prep work (researching your case and your company's policies and financial position) here are a few tips on actually having that conversation with your boss.

Avoid Assumptions by Asking the Right Questions

Successful negotiation is not just about being willing to ask for what you want but also approaching your "ask" strategically. A poor strategy is approaching negotia-tions one-dimensionally, focusing only on your own de-sired outcomes. Instead, you should take a collaborative approach, building a clear bridge between your boss's concerns and your request. The best way to do this is to prepare to pose a few open questions that explore your boss's view of the world. When formulating these ques-tions, be curious about how to make your request a win-win. For example, you might try using phrases that imply joint success, such as:

- "How do we both do well?"

- "How would you define success?"

- "How can we turn this into a win for you?"

However, in keeping your boss's perspective in mind, don't spend too much time listening passively or go overboard with the questioning. The key is to find the perfect balance between listening and asking questions, ultimately steering the discussion toward an answer.

Gather Context Through Open Dialogue

Getting the lay of the land directly from your manager before asking for what you want can help you formulate a better strategy. Initiate an open dialogue tailored to the specific points you plan to soon negotiate. For example, if you're targeting a promotion, you might ask something like, "Now that I've been in this role for two years, what actions would it take to advance to the next level?"

This type of question can open the door to the possibility of your boss revealing valuable information that could guide your future negotiation. For example, your boss may tell you that there is currently a freeze on promotions, but it's an avenue that can be explored in six months. In that case, you'll know that the timing is wrong to negotiate for a promotion right now, so you can shift gears to ask for something else or pose other questions to help you gather the information you need to improve your chances of getting what you want down the road. For example, some questions you might next ask include:

- "Assuming things are different six months from now, what are my chances of gaining a promotion?"

- "What specifically do I need to do to achieve this goal?"

- "Are there stretch assignments that I can take on over the next six months to prepare me for advancement?"

Then follow your boss's guidance, and commit to revisiting the topic in six months for a reevaluation of the timing.

Use "What If" Responses

One way to build on your boss's responses during the open dialogue stage is to have some "what if" responses ready to go. "What if" responses give you a way to further the conversation by suggesting specific actions that you might take when your boss makes a general suggestion. For example, if your boss says that you need more cross-functional experience before you can advance, you might reply with an exact strategy that you could implement to get that experience, such as:

- "What if I work directly with the marketing department on the Johnson campaign?"

- "What if I take the lead in sharing our communications strategy with the sales team?"

- "What if I shadow the distribution team lead for a week or participate in a one-day role swap with a peer in the finance department?

Involving your boss in your request using the "what if" tactic will help gain his or her buy-in and commitment with a tangible plan that can be tracked and monitored.

Let the Conversation Evolve

Even if you execute a perfect ask, there may be circumstances beyond your control that cause your boss to reject your request. Don't become so fixated on achieving your ultimate goal that you leave possible chips on the table. Keep an eye out for viable backup plans that emerge as the conversation unfolds. Even if you get a no response to your original request, you can still leave the negotiation with a small win that may put you on the path to an eventual yes. Your goal should be to avoid ending up in a position where the response is a final no.

For example, if you ask for a salary bump, proving through your internal and external market research why you deserve one, yet your boss responds that there's no budget for raises in the department currently, you might shift the conversation to requesting an extra week of vacation, more flexibility in your job, a benefit option, or paid continuing education in an area that supports your career goals.

Even if you accept a plan B as a result of your current negotiation with your boss, that's no reason to give up completely on what you really want. If your manager denies your request the first time, it doesn't necessarily mean that no is the final answer.

No matter your perceived level of expertise in negotiation or which style you use to go about it, there is power in simply moving beyond your nervousness and starting a conversation with your boss about what you want. By doing so, you'll begin to build both your skill level and your confidence, preparing you for future negotiations.

———————————

Rebecca Shambaugh is an internationally recognized leadership expert, author, and keynote speaker. She is the president of SHAMBAUGH, a global leadership development organization, and the founder of Women in Leadership and Learning (WILL).

CHAPTER 19

Negotiate for Yourself When People Don't Expect You To

by Deborah M. Kolb and Debra A. Noumair

When managers negotiate with their bosses or colleagues, they do so in the context of how (or whether) they have negotiated before. They fall back into the roles they've traditionally played, and their counterparts expect that they will act as they have in the past.

In the leadership development programs that we run for female executives at leading corporations, we use the

---

Adapted from "How to Negotiate for Yourself When People Don't Expect You To" on hbr.org, June 17, 2016 (product #H02YKF)

term "Velcro" to describe these patterns of behavior, because like Velcro, they can lock people into a weaker negotiating position that undermines their career growth
and success.

Velcro can take many forms. Some of the women we've
worked with describe being stuck in the informal role of
great producer, someone who is willing to take on ever
more work even if it's no longer relevant to their current position. Others have reputations as *fixers*, enlisted
to clean up problems but without ever getting full credit
for the work. Others are known as *team players*, who
do whatever is asked of them for the good of the group,
without ever asking how or if they will be compensated.

Recognizing one's Velcro is the first step in breaking
away from it. The second step is to know when people are
giving you an "invitation to your Velcro" and responding
in a way that puts you in a stronger negotiating position.

Consider a case study. Rebecca is a director in the
technology division of a major financial firm. Over the
past few months she spearheaded the development of
a business case for a major transformation in her division and was therefore invited to apply for a VP role
that would involve her overseeing the transition. When
the company's leaders appointed an outsider instead of
Rebecca to the job, her boss offered her a retention bonus to prove that the firm still appreciated her work.

But Rebecca recognized this was an invitation to her
team player Velcro. Her boss expected her to gratefully
accept the bonus she'd been offered, welcome her new
manager, and allow the organization to move ahead with
the transformation. This time, Rebecca wanted to break

away from that role she'd always played, to unlock her Velcro, and negotiate on her own behalf. Here's how she did it.

- **She evaluated her leverage.** Because Rebecca had played such a big role in conceiving the change initiative, her knowledge would be critical to the new VP. Her boss continually talked about how valuable she was and implied how much he needed her. This gave her the confidence to balk at the retention bonus.

- **She set the tone for the conversation.** In the past, Rebecca's immediate response to praise or a bonus would have been to thank her boss for the offer and his support. This time, to break away from her Velcro, she sat silently—a negotiation technique she'd learned in our program—and then she declined the bonus.

- **She was clear about what she wanted.** Rebecca wanted her organization to make a long-term investment in her, not a one-time payout—a raise, not a bonus—and she told her boss exactly that. He responded with all the reasons why he couldn't give her a raise (it had not been budgeted for, it was the wrong time of year), which was another invitation to her team player Velcro, but Rebecca resisted.

- **She stood firm.** Rebecca knew her boss very well and anticipated that he would keep returning to the bonus, clearly expecting that he could wear her down. He offered to discuss her development, but she said she was not interested. She repeated that the bonus was only a token recognition; she wanted validation of her value. Finally, after securing the relevant approvals, her boss agreed to give her a significant raise worth more than double the value of the bonus.

When you recognize your Velcro, you understand how you have trained people to expect you to act and how to reset those expectations so you can negotiate for more compensation, credit and resources.

————————

Deborah M. Kolb is the Deloitte Ellen Gabriel Professor for Women in Leadership (emerita) and a cofounder of the Center for Gender in Organizations at Simmons College School of Management. An expert on negotiation and leadership, she is also codirector of the Negotiations in the Workplace Project at the Program on Negotiation at Harvard Law School. She is a coauthor (with Jessica L. Porter) of *Negotiating at Work: Turn Small Wins into Big Gains*. **Debra A. Noumair** is a professor in the social-organizational psychology program and the founder and director of the Executive Masters Program in Change Leadership in the Department of Organization and Leadership at Teachers College, Columbia University.

CHAPTER 20

How to Respond When You're Asked to Help

by Deborah M. Kolb and Jessica L. Porter

More often than not, women are the ones who help others when asked. They plan the meetings, take the notes, and assume other types of "office housework," to use sociologist and business author Rosabeth Moss Kanter's immortal phrase. These thankless-but-necessary tasks keep organizations humming. But as Facebook COO Sheryl Sandberg and Wharton professor Adam Grant note in their *New York Times* article "Madame CEO, Get Me Coffee," while women are expected to do more

Adapted from "'Office Housework' Gets in Women's Way" on hbr.org, April 16, 2015 (product #H020J5)

of this work, they don't get credit for it and suffer back-lash when they refuse to do it. "When a woman declines to help a colleague, people like her less and her career suffers," they write, citing different studies by professors Madeline Heilman, Joan C. Williams, and Joyce K. Fletcher. "But when a man says no, he faces no backlash. A man who doesn't help is 'busy'; a woman is 'selfish.'"

Office "housework" is often invisible, and so its value to a team is underappreciated. That fact creates one of the hidden barriers that can keep women from ascending to more-senior leadership roles. In our decades studying this phenomenon, we've found four negotiation strategies that work.

- **Turn a request for help into a negotiation.** Alexandra, a project manager, was asked by her boss to support a leader who was having family issues and needed help doing his work. Her boss asked her to be an "acting director." Alexandra negotiated this request into a promotion: She agreed to help, as long as she would be named to a true director role after the helping period ended and the leader returned to his job.

- **Ascertain the cost of your contribution.** Helping is not a free good. Not only does it take time away from your day job, but it can also exact a toll on your health and family. When Patria, a program leader in an NGO, was asked by her director to help a colleague whose team was having trouble managing its workload, she agreed. But when she factored in the additional time required to help her colleague, her prorated hourly pay dropped dramatically. When she pointed this out to the director in stark dollar terms, Patria was able to negotiate for more resources in order to continue to help without putting in more time.

- **Demonstrate the value of your help.** In our work, we have seen how women successfully incorporate their helping time into an expanded version of their jobs by showing the value of what they're doing. That is what Isobel, a communications manager, did. After initially helping another division with a government client and saving an important relationship, the other division kept asking for her "fixing" help. Although she liked being seen as a fixer, she knew she could not continue doing it and still keep up with her job. By showing the value of her work to the other division, she negotiated the fixing work she was doing into a new expanded role, with a commensurate title and raise.

- **If the ask is more personal than professional, build in reciprocity.** In the examples above, helping benefited the organization. But getting the coffee and planning the office party are more personal. When negotiating around these types of requests, ask for reciprocity: If I do this, then what will you do? Allison, a senior leader, was always willing to take her turn getting the coffee—with the provision "I'll do it today, and next time it will be your turn." And she made sure the other person remembered.

Negotiating the conditions of your help is good for you as an individual and good for your organization. When you help without conditions, you train people to expect that you will continue to do so. But when you negotiate the conditions of your help, it can be a small win for you. And as we have found in our work, these small wins can start to accumulate into bigger gains. Sandberg and Grant note that it doesn't have to be the case that "no good deed goes unpunished." But reversing that behavior requires women to place value on their help and to negotiate to have that work acknowledged and rewarded.

Deborah M. Kolb is the Deloitte Ellen Gabriel Professor for Women in Leadership (emerita) and a cofounder of the Center for Gender in Organizations at Simmons College School of Management. An expert on negotiation and leadership, she is also a codirector of the Negotiations in the Workplace Project at the Program on Negotiation at Harvard Law School. **Jessica L. Porter** advises organizations worldwide on gender and leadership. As a researcher, Porter has led influential investigations into effective work habits and creating change. Kolb and Porter are the coauthors of *Negotiating at Work: Turn Small Wins into Big Gains*.

Navigate Difficult Situations

CHAPTER 21

How Stay-at-Home Parents Can Transition Back to Work

by Dorie Clark

The vast majority of people who take time off to raise children (or other caregiving work) would ultimately like to return to the workplace. But transitioning back isn't so easy. Research by the Center for Talent Innovation shows that only 73% of highly qualified women who wanted to return to work were able to do so, and just 40% of those landed a regular full-time job.[1] What's the problem, and how can you overcome it?

Adapted from content posted on hbr.org, April 24, 2017 (product #H03KZI)

One of the biggest challenges professionals face in the midst of a career transition is managing their brand and how they're perceived. For legal reasons, hiring managers can't openly say what may be on their minds: that you might be a less committed or effective worker now that you're a parent and have a gap in your résumé.

Unfortunately, when a bias is unspoken, it's much harder to address outright. That's why it's on you to proactively address their concerns and show them why they're unfounded. Here's how to do it.

Show That Your Skills Are Current

Depending how long you were out of the workforce, potential employers might worry that you're out of touch. You may have had stellar experience in marketing, for instance, but if you left your job in 2006, you've missed the entirety of the social media era, and an employer might be justified in wondering if you've kept up. Go out of your way to prove them wrong.

Make sure you have a robust LinkedIn profile, and consider using other public social media platforms, such as Twitter, to share posts regularly about your industry and show that you've kept pace with industry trends. In your cover letter and interviews, be sure to cite any germane volunteer experience. If you helped organize major fundraisers for your child's school or led a search committee for your favorite charity's new executive director, those skills are eminently transferable.

That was the strategy Naomi Press followed. A former banker who took 20 years out of the workforce, Press stayed very active in her children's school. "In truth, running the parents' association was a lot like having a full-time job (without the paycheck)," she says, "so I could talk about my responsibilities in that position and the valuable skills I honed: project management, people management, writing, editing, marketing, and so on." She leveraged those skills—which melded education and business savvy—into a new job as the assistant director of a university program.

Keep Your Network Current

Volunteer experience is great, but it may not be enough. "If I were going to land a job," Press surmised, "it would likely be through networking. I didn't think my volunteer experience would necessarily convince a random hiring manager that I deserved to get an interview."

Nancy Park, who recently returned to work at her old company after a five-year break to raise her children, also credits networking with a successful transition. During her time out of the workforce, she stayed in the loop by meeting with her former colleagues every few months and ultimately heard about an opening—which became her new job—from them.

Explain Why You're Returning to the Workforce

The hiring manager may have two unspoken concerns:

- Does this candidate really *want* to be here?

- Does the person have childcare figured out, or will they get called away all the time if their kid is sick?

You need to allay the manager's concerns proactively and explain why you're applying for this job at this moment. In truth, the need to earn more money might be a factor. But don't go there, because they'll wonder if you'll bolt at the first sign of a higher paycheck from another firm. Instead, stress that you're eager to return to the workforce so you can make a contribution (and how, specifically, you'd like to do so at their company) and that you're now in a position to reenter because your caregiving responsibilities have lightened (perhaps your kids have started school, you've hired a nanny, or your children are older now and need less supervision). That information shows you'll be a motivated employee and won't be more distracted by personal obligations than anyone else.

Reposition Your "Weakness" as a Strength

It's easy to imagine that your time off work is a weakness; after all, others have been amassing new professional skills and getting promoted while you were on another track entirely. Indeed, hiring managers may well view it that way. But you can't simply accept that frame and apologize for your choices ("I know I don't have as much recent experience as the other candidates, but . . .").

Indeed, as Park notes, returning to work after time off may be challenging, but so is any kind of change, whether it's switching firms or moving to a new role. "Don't overestimate the impact of being out for some period," she says. "If you were a high performer before and have strong skills and renewed drive to work hard, you can absolutely still add value to a company."

Plus, parenting has almost certainly taught you important lessons about multitasking, negotiation, persuasion, and stress management—and that may, in fact, make you a more productive and well-rounded employee. Research by the Federal Reserve Bank of St. Louis indicates that while working mothers do experience a productivity dip when their children are small, they actually outpace the productivity of childless women over the course of their careers—likely because they've learned how to rigorously maximize their efficiency.[2] Own those skills, and position them as an asset rather than a weakness because they are.

Don't Get Discouraged

Even if you've been following all of these steps, success doesn't come instantly. Park recalls that it took about a year between deciding to reenter the workforce and finding the right position and describes the process as "moderately difficult." But with time and patience, she landed an exciting opportunity. In the interim, you might consider taking on low-paid (or unpaid) assignments, if you're confident they'll lead to new skills or an enhanced network. In my book *Reinventing You*, I profile Susan Leeds, whose interest in environmental issues prompted her to sign on for a two-year nonprofit fellowship (and a huge pay cut). But the experience and connections ultimately led to a fruitful new career running a public-private environmental partnership.

It's unfair—but common—for talented professionals to be penalized for taking time off for caregiving. If you want to return to the workforce, you have to manage and overcome the unspoken assumptions about who you are and what you're capable of. By making it clear that your skills are current, networking assiduously, showing that you're motivated, and demonstrating that your caregiving experience is actually a strength, you can go a long way toward combatting pernicious stereotypes and reentering professional life on your own terms.

———————

Dorie Clark is a keynote speaker and an adjunct professor at Duke University's Fuqua School of Business. She is the author of *Reinventing You* (Harvard Business Review Press, 2013) and *Entrepreneurial You* (Harvard Business Review Press, 2017).

NOTES

1. Sylvia Ann Hewlett and Carolyn Buck Luce, "As Career Paths Change, Make On-Ramping Easy," hbr.org, July 8, 2010, https://hbr.org/2010/07/as-careers-paths-change-make-o.

2. Matthias Krapf, Heinrich W. Ursprung, and Christian Zimmermann, "Parenthood and Productivity of Highly Skilled Labor: Evidence from the Groves of Academe," working paper 2014-001A, Federal Reserve Bank of St. Louis, St. Louis, Missouri, January 2014, https://files.stlouisfed.org/files/htdocs/wp/2014/2014-001.pdf.

CHAPTER 22

How to React to a Biased Performance Review

by Paola Cecchi-Dimeglio and Kim Kleman

We're all familiar with bias in performance reviews. Whether it's the halo-or-horn effect, where the manager's overall favorable or negative opinion of an employee colors their entire assessment, or the so-called recency bias, where the employee's latest behavior overshadows earlier actions, many employees feel they have been rated unfairly during their evaluation.

But women, especially, are subject to biased performance reviews—and this is the case whether their manager is male or female. According to research conducted by one of us (Paola) working with large domestic and international professional services firms and using content analysis of individual annual performance reviews, women are 40% more likely to receive critical subjective feedback or vague feedback during their review, as opposed to either positive or critical objective feedback. And their performance is more likely to be attributed to characteristics such as luck or their ability to spend long hours in the office (perceived as real commitment to the firm), rather than their abilities and skills. As such, they often don't receive due credit for their work.

What's more, they're more often held to a double standard—criticized for the same attributes that men are praised for. "Heidi seems to shrink when she's around others, and especially around clients, she needs to be more self-confident," a manager wrote in one of the many company reviews that Paola has analyzed. But a similar problem—confidence in working with clients— was given a positive spin when a man was struggling with it: "Jim needs to develop his natural ability to work with people."

In another pair of reviews, the reviewer highlighted the woman's "analysis paralysis," while the same behavior in a male colleague was seen as careful thoughtfulness: "Simone seems paralyzed and confused when facing tight deadlines to make decisions," while "Cameron seems hesitant in making decisions, yet he is able to work out multiple alternative solutions and determine the most suitable one."

So what should you do if this happens to you? You could accept the evaluation at face value and question your competence. You could begin looking for work else-where. Or you could dispute the evaluation, reacting an-grily and defensively in the moment.

But responding in those ways won't get you anywhere. Instead, consider two alternatives: Start a conversation with your manager to understand how you were rated and what they might have overlooked, and make a plan of action so that next time, you avoid this situation and are recognized for exceeding expectations.

How to React

When you're in a performance review meeting with your boss that you feel is unfair, remain calm. Use the following tips to better understand your manager's evaluation and what it was based on.

Listen—really listen

Seek to understand exactly what your boss is saying. You're trying to figure out the metrics your manager used to evaluate you. Ideally, metrics are SMART—specific, measurable, achievable, realistic, and time bound—based on goals that were established at the beginning of the evaluation cycle. But not all workplaces have these strict definitions. If expectations were fuzzier, aim to understand what metrics your boss did use to assess your performance.

Dig for more details

Ask questions. Phrase them in a way that suggests you're trying to understand, not second-guess, your manager's assessment. For example, a common scenario for women is to get penalized for taking too long on a project—when no deadline had been set. In a situation like this, you might respond, "You say that I took too long to complete project X. What was the time frame you were looking for? How could I have done this differently?"

Ask about a similar project that you know to have been led by a male colleague. Was your boss happier with that project? How long did it take to complete? What did that team leader do that your manager wishes you did? You don't want to expressly state that you believe your boss is gender biased. But these questions can help reveal that maybe you aren't held to the same standard as your male colleague.

Research and follow up

At the end of the conversation, tell your boss that the evaluation surprised you and that you'd like to talk again. Don't rush that next conversation; you need to give yourself time to calm down. But try to schedule it within a week or two of the first one. During that time, review your notes about the projects your boss focused on, and ask your teammates for their thoughts about your performance.

Keep in mind that you're not asking your teammates to go to bat for you against your boss. Nor are you seeking ammunition for every comment and criticism in your review. You want to know what your colleagues honestly thought about working with you and how you could have performed better.

When framing the question to your colleagues consider the following rules: Identify a specific situation (the beginning, middle, and end of project X, for example), a specific behavior (problem solving or communicating, for instance) and its impact on others (related to collaboration, deadlines, and so on). Ask them to be candid and to tell you what you can do better going forward. Listen without judgment, and write down what they say. You'll get a lot of detailed feedback.

When you do meet with your manager again, come prepared with examples and talking points that speak to the metrics your boss has cited, including some of the feedback that your colleagues shared with you. Tell your manager, too, that you understand there's room for improvement in your performance. Research shows that people who engage in blatant self-promotion tend to put others off, but those who have open and productive dialogues are more likely to have their viewpoints heard.[1]

Don't demand a reevaluation, but ask your manager if the appraisal can be revised to reflect your manager's insights and some of your information, too, so it communicates a fuller picture. If your boss says yes, terrific! If the answer is no, then you've at least let your manager know that you take your evaluation seriously and that you're eager to improve. Then you can take steps to avoid such an assessment again.

Looking Ahead

How can you set yourself up to receive a better appraisal next year? Based on the results of a field experiment that Paola performed at an international professional service provider, we've discovered an effective exercise women

can do throughout the year to make sure that their contributions are noticed and evaluated fairly.

At the beginning of every project, write several brief
paragraphs describing its scope and your role in it. Here
are some specifics to include:

- **Define your responsibilities for the task.** If you're
  the lead infographic designer on a job and your
  team is responsible for the design that will be the
  centerpiece of a client presentation, the junior
  consultant in charge of managing the presentation might help you highlight the key content, but
  you have authority over the design of individual
  elements.

- **Identify who has the final authority.** You and the
  junior consultant are charged with producing the
  content, but the lead senior consultant is responsible for how the whole presentation and infograph-
  ics work together.

- **Determine outside resources to be consulted.**
  Perhaps specific charts require discussion with
  subject-matter experts outside your team.

- **Clarify who needs status updates and how often
  they need them.** For instance, the lead senior
  consultant and the partner in charge of the client
  relationship will need to be updated weekly.

Use this document as a personal roadmap, so you are
reminded of everyone's roles and responsibilities, as well
as whom you should keep informed. Then, at the end of
the project, summarize key points: what went well and

what you believe needed to improve based on the feedback you received during the work. Also, seek specific feedback from your project teammates. What could you do better next time? How could they simplify their work during the next project?

You don't need to share these documents and feedback with others, but they should communicate what you've learned and how it is influencing your work. At the onset of the next project, let your teammates know that you are implementing changes based on their recommendations.

Last, right before performance appraisal time, send a short note to all the colleagues you've worked with on various projects throughout the year. In a few paragraphs, recap the project deliverables, the project's tasks and challenges, and how you overcame them. Include what you learned from your colleagues' advice and how it benefitted your professional development throughout the year. In doing this, you remind your colleagues of all you've contributed in the past year, so they can keep this in mind in 360 reviews or if asked for feedback from your manager. (If your company doesn't have 360-degree reviews or your manager isn't part of the process, make sure they get a version of this project summary as well.)

The advantage of adopting this proactive approach is that it makes you more visible to colleagues and managers and includes them in your success. It also reduces the halo-or-horn effect and the recency bias described earlier. Moreover, colleagues and managers feel heard when they see that you've acted on their advice and represent it to the leaders above you.

Even better, with this approach colleagues will rate you much more similarly to how they rate men. You'll receive better reviews and will be more recognized for your accomplishments. And your future evaluations will be three times less likely to show gender bias.

———————

Paola Cecchi-Dimeglio, JD, LLM, PhD, is a behavioral scientist and the chair of the Executive Leadership Research Initiative for Women and Minority Attorneys at the Center for the Legal Profession at Harvard Law School and a senior research fellow at HLS and at Harvard Kennedy School (WAPPP). She is also the CEO of PCD Consulting Group, a leading consulting firm dedicated to solving business and policy challenges related to gender using behavioral science, behavioral economics, big data, and artificial intelligence. Reach her at paola @paolacecchidimeglio.com and follow her on Twitter @HLSPaola. **Kim Kleman** is the former editor in chief of *The American Lawyer* and *Consumer Reports* magazines and teaches journalism at the Columbia University Graduate School of Journalism. Reach her at kdkleman @gmail.com and follow her on Twitter @kdkleman.

NOTE

1. See C. A. Moss-Racusin and L. A. Rudman, "Disruptions in Women's Self-Promotion: The Backlash Avoidance Model," *Psychology of Women Quarterly* 34, no. 2 (2010): 186–202 and H. R. Bowles, L. Babcock, and K. L. McGinn, "Constraints and Triggers: Situational Mechanics of Gender in Negotiation," *Journal of Personality and Social Psychology* 89, no. 6 (2005): 951–965.

CHAPTER 23

Responding to an Offensive Comment at Work

by Amy Gallo

Your colleague says something that immediately makes you feel uncomfortable. He thinks he's just being funny, but the comment is inappropriate—maybe even sexist or racist. What should you say or do if you find yourself in this situation? Is there a way to draw attention to the comment without putting the other person on the defensive? And are you risking your reputation, job, or career by speaking up?

Adapted from "How to Respond to an Offensive Comment at Work" on hbr.org, February 8, 2017 (product #H03FZP)

What the Experts Say

There's no denying that this situation is a tough one. Joan Williams, founding director of the Center for WorkLife Law at UC Hastings College of the Law, says that these decisions are particularly risky because they involve "two of the most corrosive elements of bias in the workplace": the uncertainty of knowing whether what you heard is bias and the fear that you might be penalized for how you handle it. It's normal to question ourselves in these cases, wondering if we heard the person right or if it was just a joke.

Even if you think you would say something in the situation, in reality you might not. Research by Alexander Czopp, director of the Center for Cross-Cultural Research at Western Washington University, and his colleagues show that there is a "discrepancy between what people predict they would do and what they actually do." Here's some advice for the next time a colleague says something offensive.

Weigh the benefits of speaking up against the costs

The first step is to decide whether it's worth addressing the comment. There are certainly good reasons to do so. Preserving your own sense of integrity and ridding the workplace of racism are laudable goals, Williams notes. "If you don't speak up, you're signaling that this is OK. You've essentially just given the person permission to do it again." This might also be an opportunity to change your colleague's behavior for the better—a chance you don't want to miss. Czopp's research shows that "addressing offensive behavior in the right way in the moment can change it in the future."

If you're in a position of power, the stakes are higher. Managers have a responsibility (in some cases, a legal one) to make sure no one feels threatened or uncomfortable at work, and studies show that you have more influence if you are not the subject of the bias, says Williams. "When it comes to sexism, for example, men tend to be more persuasive when confronting people," she says. "We afford them more credibility because it's not their 'game.'"

Williams adds that you need to consider whom you're dealing with, what their reaction might be, and what the political costs will be if you call them out. They might be dismissive ("You're overreacting. It was just a joke") or defensive ("What are you accusing me of?"). So ask yourself: How does this person normally react to being challenged? Are they generally self-aware? Well-intended?

You'll also want to consider the person's authority over you and whether they're likely to penalize you for speaking up. "Your job security or personal safety may be at risk," says Czopp. This is especially true if you're part of a group that's already subject to bias. Williams's research shows that women and people of color get more pushback when they're assertive. That's not to say you shouldn't speak up, but you should be realistic about the consequences of doing so. If your ultimate aim is to keep your job, you may decide to keep quiet.

Don't make assumptions

If you decide to say something, approach the situation as if the person didn't mean to offend you. Most of the time, "the person is just clueless and doesn't know how their behavior is being interpreted," Williams explains. Be compassionate; chances are, you've made mistakes too. "Have we all made stupid comments? Sure. You're not perfect either," says Williams. You might even share your own experience of saying something you later wished you could take back. Explaining that you've been in similar situations may make the person less defensive and more open to hearing your perspective.

Be careful not to level accusations. Czopp's research shows that harsh statements, such as "That's racist," resulted in much more defensive reactions. He says that most people have an "exaggerated view" of what these terms mean, so they react strongly. "We think of white supremacists, the KKK, and cross burning—anything that implies that we're on the same continuum as those things is upsetting." Williams agrees: "It might feel righteous to call people out, but no one wants to hear that they're being sexist, racist, or otherwise offensive."

Instead of labeling the comment as offensive, Williams and Czopp both advise explaining how it makes you feel. You might say, "I know it wasn't your intent, but that made me uncomfortable" or "I'm confused by what you said." Don't think of this as sidestepping the issue, Czopp says. Instead, you're handling the matter delicately. It's an approach that is "more likely to change their behavior in future situations."

Engage in discussion

Williams suggests following your initial statement with a question like, "What did you mean by that comment?" or "What information are you basing that on?" By having a conversation with the person, you can help them explore their biases and clear up any possible misunderstandings. You might even ask them to repeat what they said. This will prompt them to think through what they meant by the remark, as well as its effect on others, and give them a chance to take it back.

If the person doesn't think their comment was offensive, you can help educate them by offering an observation or more information. For example, if the person suggested that your female colleague is slacking off by leaving work early, you might say something like: "I read an interesting study the other day that found that when working moms leave the office, we assume they're taking care of their kids. But when working dads leave the office, we don't even notice." It's important to do this in a way that isn't passive-aggressive. The more genuine you are about sharing information and not trapping the person in their bias, the more likely they are to hear you.

Try alternative approaches

If you decide that you're not comfortable addressing the comment, there are other things you can do, says Czopp. For example, you might change the subject, sending a subtle message to the person that you disapprove of the remark. "You have to rely on the person's emotional intelligence to pick up on the cue," he says. You might also wait and see what happens. Sometimes the person who made the comment will realize their mistake and apologize.

Or just call it out

Depending on the severity of the offense, you may decide you're not concerned about the other person's sense of self, says William: "You may feel that you need to just call it out." And that's fine as long as you've weighed the costs. If the person gets their hackles up and becomes defensive, "you've now got another piece of information about who that person is," says Williams.

Appeal to someone in authority

If the comments continue and you feel uncomfortable, you might consider escalating the issue. Williams says there is power in numbers. "Can you find others who have been offended and make the case that the person is creating a hostile climate? If you've tried to deal with it on your own and haven't had success, you can privately bring it to a senior person." You might say something like: "A whole group of us are having this experience, and we'd like your advice." Just keep in mind, warns Williams, that as you ratchet it up, you expend more political capital.

Principles to Remember

Do:

- Weigh the consequences of *not* speaking up. Leaving a comment unaddressed may give the person permission to do the same thing again.

- Recognize that if you are in a position of power, you have a responsibility to address offensive comments.

- Ask questions that help the person reflect on what they said and clear up any misunderstandings.

Don't:

- Neglect to think through the political costs, especially if you're the target of the comment.

- Assume the person meant to offend you or anyone else; it's possible that they are clueless.

- Accuse someone of being biased. That's likely to put them on the defensive and unlikely to change their behavior over the long term.

Amy Gallo is a contributing editor at *Harvard Business Review* and the author of the *HBR Guide to Dealing with Conflict* (Harvard Business Review Press, 2017). She writes and speaks about workplace dynamics. Follow her on Twitter @amyegallo.

CHAPTER 24

What to Do If You've Been Sexually Harassed

by Joanna L. Grossman and Deborah L. Rhode

Sexual harassment scandals at major companies such as Uber and Fox News have been a reminder not only that sexual harassment is still a regrettably routine feature of working life but also that even some of the most powerful perpetrators can, eventually, be held accountable.

Despite more than four decades of legal sanctions and workplace training, harassing conduct remains persistent and pervasive. We have written elsewhere about

---

Adapted from "Understanding Your Legal Options If You've Been Sexually Harassed" on hbr.org, June 22, 2017 (product #H03QA6)

how the law and workplace need to change to better address the problem. Our focus here is on what women, who reportedly make up 90% of harassment targets, can do when they confront it personally and what strategies are most likely to be effective.

The most critical questions for employees who have been harassed at work are, first, what response do they want? And second, what are they prepared to risk to get it?

For most women, the answers are likely to depend on the seriousness of the harassment and the costs of complaining. Is the conduct ongoing, a threat to personal safety or well-being, or likely to have major job or career consequences? How easy would it be to avoid the harassment? For example, in a lawsuit against UC Berkeley School of Law, the dean's assistant complained that her boss had repeatedly hugged and kissed her. The conduct occurred almost daily, and the assistant had no way to remove herself from the situation without quitting. Some of the allegations against Fox News chair Roger Ailes involved women who were not under his ongoing supervision but who wanted jobs that he could deny them if they didn't submit to his sexual demands. As he allegedly told one of them, "You know if you want to play with the big boys, you have to lay with the big boys." These women paid a significant career price for refusing, but at least they had the opportunity to avoid the harassment by staying in their current positions. By contrast, the dean's assistant had little choice but to complain if she wanted to hold on to her position and stop the harassment.

Another key consideration for women deciding how to respond to harassment is how much legal or professional leverage they have. This depends both on whether they are likely to prevail in a lawsuit and whether their public disclosures can cause significant reputational damage.

To evaluate their legal claims, women need to understand certain basic facts about the law governing sexual harassment. The United States Supreme Court has held that Title VII of the Civil Rights Act of 1964, which bans employment discrimination on the basis of sex (as well as race, color, ethnicity, national origin, and religion), includes a ban on sexual harassment and provides that employers can be held liable for unlawful harassment in certain circumstances. Most state laws extend similar protections. Two Supreme Court cases from 1998, *Faragher v. Boca Raton* and *Burlington Industries, Inc. v. Ellerth*, established a framework for accountability based on the nature of the harassment and the position of the harasser. Employers are strictly liable for harassment by a supervisor that results in a tangible employment action. An example would be a manager who fires a subordinate for refusing to sleep with him. For harassment that does not result in such a tangible action, employers can avoid liability by establishing an affirmative defense. In effect, they must show that they took reasonable measures to prevent and correct harassment *and* that the victim failed to take advantage of opportunities to avoid harm. In theory, the burden is on the employer to show why liability is *not* appropriate, rather than the converse. In practice, however, courts have time and again granted employers the benefit of the affirmative defense without ever inquiring whether the measures they took to prevent or respond to harassment were effective. That may change in response to the shift in cultural norms accompanying the #MeToo movement. But women should be aware that traditionally, the law has too often given employers a safe harbor.

Women who are considering making a formal complaint should be realistic about the financial, psychological, and reputational cost of pursuing it. Defendants typically have deeper pockets than victims, and the price of hiring a lawyer is often prohibitive. To be sure, attorneys specializing in harassment cases are often willing to work on a contingent fee, which means that their compensation comes only if they win a judgment for the complainant. But unless damages and the likelihood of recovery are substantial, few lawyers will want to take the case. Employment discrimination cases have the lowest win rate for plaintiffs of any civil cause of action. And in sexual harassment cases it is the complainant as much as the harasser who is on trial. Consider the experience of Gretchen Carlson, the first woman to go public with a claim against Roger Ailes. The public relations department of Fox initially sought to shoot the messenger. It portrayed Carlson as a disgruntled employee with an ax to grind, released affectionate emails from Carlson to Ailes, and recruited other women at Fox News to come to his defense.

While this may sound daunting, there are steps that targets of harassment can take to anticipate and mitigate these kinds of challenges.

First, employees who experience harassment should make a record. They should keep copies of incriminating emails and voicemails, and they should document their own efforts to stop the abuse. If their organization has confidential reporting channels, they should use them and, if they fear retaliation, consider the possibility of making an anonymous complaint and collecting any evidence of retaliation. They should also tell trusted friends and family members about any harassing or retaliatory conduct so those individuals could serve as witnesses in a subsequent investigation or legal proceeding.

Even if the employee is convinced that reporting the incident will do nothing, she should still report it. Courts typically ask whether the victim filed an internal complaint, and if she didn't, why not. If she waited to complain, they ask why and for how long and are unwilling to accept the most obvious and compelling reasons. A delay of even a few days can be deemed "unreasonable," and fears of retaliation are frequently dismissed as too vague and "generalized" to justify the failure to complain. Courts also often require specific evidence of retaliation; a generalized fear of retaliation is not enough for victims to get a jury to agree with their claims. Fears of retaliation are typically well founded: Employees who file complaints of discrimination experience retaliation at rates as high as 50% to 60%.[1] Targets of harassment can bolster their claims by documenting specific instances of retaliatory behavior. For example, in February 2017 Susan Fowler published a blog post entitled, "Reflecting on One Very, Very Strange Year at Uber," on her website, detailing her unsuccessful efforts to halt harassment at

Uber. After repeatedly complaining about an instance of discrimination, she was threatened with termination if she filed another report. Eventually Fowler quit, but her blog recounting the experience went viral, and Uber CEO Travis Kalanick launched an "urgent investigation" into her allegations. The company subsequently fired more than 20 employees. (Kalanick later stepped down as CEO, in part because of the company's culture and his influence on it.)

This example underscores the value of going public with or without the threat of litigation. Negative publicity can sometimes be more effective in pressuring companies to take harassment seriously than reliance on formal complaint channels.

Finally, as the Uber and Fox News cases both suggest, women can work collectively to pressure employers. What enabled Carlson to prevail was the steady trickle of other victims ready to tell their stories. Fowler likewise discovered other women at Uber who had been harassed. Safety in numbers is often what empowers women to come forward. And numbers are often what forces employers to settle and take preventive action, as is clear from the ouster of Ailes, Fox News host Bill O'Reilly, and Uber employees.

After decades of research, we know quite a bit about how victims respond to harassment and why the law has so often failed to provide appropriate remedies. They wait to see whether the behavior will stop on its own, or they keep silent because they fear that reporting will be futile or that the harasser will retaliate. Rather than filing internal or external complaints, harassment targets tend to resort to informal and nonconfrontational remedies. They vent, cope, laugh it off, treat it as some kind of less-threatening misunderstanding, or simply try to get on with their jobs (and lives). They may blame themselves, pretend it isn't happening, or fall into self-destructive behaviors like developing eating disorders or engaging in excessive drinking. Many women choose costly consequences—such as quitting their jobs—to avoid dealing with harassment directly or have high levels of absenteeism that lead to termination or other adverse results.

We hope that offering concrete strategies will help more women fight back. Documenting harassment and retaliation, working collectively with other women, and publicizing abuse can all be effective. Increasing resources are available for women who experience abuse, including the Women's Law Center's matching system that links complainants with lawyers willing to take cases for free or for reduced fees.

Reforms in workplace practices are also necessary. All organizations have a responsibility to provide not just formal policies but also effective complaint channels, protections against retaliation, and efforts to monitor their progress in preventing and remedying harassment. Studies show that women respond more assertively to misconduct when employers take proactive efforts to deter harassment and protect complainants.

Those who care about equal employment opportunity can also support organizations that are working for reforms in laws governing sexual harassment and representing women who cannot afford legal assistance. And those who suffer abuse can tell their stories, through both traditional outlets and social media. The ouster of Roger Ailes and Bill O'Reilly and the shake-up at Uber make it clear that women's voices can matter. But the fact that achieving those results took a quarter century of complaints at Fox and the unrelenting glare of public scrutiny at Uber reminds us how much progress remains to be made.

———————

Joanna L. Grossman is the Ellen K. Solender Endowed Chair in Women and Law at SMU Dedman School of Law. Her most recent book is *Nine to Five: How Gender, Sex, and Sexuality Continue to Define the American Workplace*. She is a regular columnist for Justia's "Verdict." **Deborah L. Rhode** is the Ernest W. McFarland Professor of Law and the director of the Center on the Legal Profession at Stanford University. Her most recent book on gender is *Women and Leadership: The State of Play and Strategies for Change*.

NOTE

1. Deborah L. Brake and Joanna L. Grossman, "The Failure of Title VII as a Rights-Claiming System," *North Carolina Law Review* 86 (2008): 859–938.

CHAPTER 25

Older Women Are Being Forced Out of the Workforce

by Lauren Stiller Rikleen

Susan is a woman in her sixties who has spent decades working in the insurance business. After years of performance reviews describing her outstanding work ethic, her fortunes turned when she started reporting to a woman 20 years her junior. Under her new manager, Susan felt set up to fail: She was assigned more cases and held to much higher standards than her younger colleagues. Susan's manager issued a formal performance evaluation that characterized her as failing in her

---

Adapted from content posted on hbr.org, March 10, 2016 (product #H02QEA)

duties. Although Susan was supposed to have 90 days to improve, her manager fired her after a few days. Susan has since sued her employer for age discrimination.

Mary is a 72-year-old sociology professor with significant scholarship credentials, several teaching awards, and an illustrious record, including three stints as department chair. Her positive career recognition came to an end when the university hired a much younger dean, who denied her funding to hire needed full-time faculty, accused her of poor leadership, and favored her younger colleagues. The dean eventually told her that he would not approve an additional term for her to serve as department chair. Mary filed a lawsuit against the university for age discrimination, which was recently settled.

At the age of 64, Jane had worked as a bartender at a neighborhood bar for more than a decade. The bar was being sold, however, and the buyers told Jane that she was too old to be a bartender, disparaging her age and gender in front of other employees and customers before the sale was finalized. They did not keep her on and instead hired significantly younger women. Jane has since filed suit for age and gender discrimination.

Susan, Mary, and Jane (all of whom have been renamed to preserve anonymity) represent a variety of backgrounds and positions, but their stories share a theme that is both commonplace and all too often ignored: Senior women are being phased out of the workplace. For the past five years, I have traveled across the United States, speaking and conducting research on women's leadership and advancement and bias in the workplace. Hundreds of women in their fifties and sixties have shared their stories of demotion, job loss, and an inability to find another job—outcomes they attribute primarily to their age and gender. These women often have long histories of career success, but they have seen their responsibilities assigned to younger workers, their compensation lowered for inexplicable reasons, and their career mobility impaired by a workplace that seems to value youth over experience.

Many women who feel discriminated against because of their age believe that their only recourse is to sue their employers—but they have a daunting road ahead if they choose to do so. Even as state and federal laws prohibit age discrimination, a 2009 Supreme Court decision made it much harder for plaintiffs to win by shifting the burden of proof in these cases to them. This creates bookend barriers to senior women who are seeking to change jobs or reenter the workplace.

For many of the women I spoke with, these challenges arose just as they were freed from the family responsibilities that slowed their career progress when they were younger. As mothers, they were subjected to assumptions about whether their family obligations interfered with their commitment to work. And when their children grew up, they raced back into the workforce, only to see their careers stalled by a reduced tolerance for aging women at work.

This observation appears to be backed up by research. A study by economists at the University of California at Irvine and Tulane University found "robust evidence of age discrimination in hiring against older women."[1] The data show that it is harder for older women to find jobs than it is for older men.

The researchers created 40,000 job applications for fictional job seekers and submitted them to a variety of open positions posted online. They made résumés for older (ages 64–66), middle-aged (49–51), and younger (29–31) applicants. After monitoring employers' responses to these dummy applications, the researchers concluded that the evidence showed it was more difficult for older female workers to get hired. For example, the authors reported that the callback rate for middle-aged female sales applicants was lower than for younger female applicants, while callback rates for middle-aged and young male applicants were similar.

The authors suggested two possible theories for why older women may suffer from age discrimination more than older men. One is that age discrimination laws do not deal effectively with the situation of older women who face both age and gender bias. The other possibility touches on society's focus on women's physical appearance, a scrutiny that does not seem to similarly impact men. For example, this seems to be playing out in Hollywood, as actresses like Catherine Zeta-Jones and Kim Cattrall decry the industry's lack of roles for women in their forties and older.

For too long, this nexus between age and gender discrimination has been discussed in whispered anecdotes and quietly filed lawsuits. Although this study is a great step in raising the issue, it is striking how little research actually exists on the topic. In order to address and root out age and gender discrimination, there will need to be more research that scopes out the problem and offers recommendations for fixing it, and organizations have to take stock and be willing to make changes.

One in three Americans are 50 or older, and by 2030, one in five will be 65 and above.[2] As women continue to outlive men, they are more likely to have increased healthcare needs, are more likely to be widowed, and will have fewer years in the workforce to accumulate post-retirement savings and sufficient social security.[3]

Managers need to recognize and root out these biases against older women to ensure a workforce where all generations are embraced for the talents they bring. For 50 to truly become the new 30, we need a workplace that provides equal opportunities for women of all ages.

Lauren Stiller Rikleen, the author of *You Raised Us, Now Work with Us: Millennials, Career Success, and Building Strong Workplace Teams,* was named by Public Media's Next Avenue as one of the 50 most influential people in aging. As president of the Rikleen Institute for Strategic Leadership, Lauren speaks and consults on gender and generational issues in the workplace.

NOTES

1. David Neumark, Ian Burn, and Patrick Button, "Is It Harder for Older Workers to Find Jobs? New and Improved Evidence from a Field Experiment," working paper 21669, National Bureau of Economic Research, Cambridge, MA, October 2015, http://www.nber .org/papers/w21669.

2. "The Demographics of Aging," Transgenerational Design Matters, http://transgenerational.org/aging/demographics.htm.

3. "Ageing Societies: The Benefits, and the Costs, of Living Longer," *World of Work: The Magazine of the International Labor Organization,* December 1, 2009, http://www.ilo.org/global/publica tions/world-of-work-magazine/articles/WCM_041965/lang--en/ index.htm.

Advice for Leaders and Managers

CHAPTER 26

Reframe Diversity by Teaching Inclusivity to All

by Avivah Wittenberg-Cox

Deloitte has started a major debate in diversity circles by turning its approach upside down. The firm is ending its women's network and other affinity groups and starting to focus on . . . men. The central idea: It'll offer all managers—including the white guys who still dominate leadership—the skills to become more inclusive, then hold them accountable for building more-balanced businesses.

"A lot of our leaders are still older white men, and they need to be part of the conversation and advocate for women," is how Deepa Purushothaman, national

Adapted from "Deloitte's Radical Attempt to Reframe Diversity" on hbr.org, August 3, 2017 (product #H03TRY)

director of Deloitte's soon-to-be-disbanded women's employee resource group (ERG), puts it.[1]

This is a reversal from the strategy large companies have been trying for decades: focusing on empowering "out groups" through dedicated networks, such as ERGs or other so-called "affinity groups." This approach was pioneered in 1970 when Xerox launched the first such group, now called the National Black Employees Association. Today many large companies have ERGs for employees of color, LGBTQ employees, women, and so on. The idea was to help these groups feel more engaged in corporate cultures created and dominated by straight white men. Out-group employees would gain confidence and help each other. Their concerns could more easily be heard and addressed. The groups would also offer easy, in-house access to insights into different customer segments.

It was a well-intentioned and—to be fair—pretty radical idea in 1970. Some of those aims were achieved. But the overarching objective and promise of these groups never quite materialized: that they would help out-group employees reach the top echelons of leadership. This goal was never reached in part because of a flawed underlying assumption that the ERGs' unspoken purpose was to help out-groups figure out how to assimilate, and assimilation was a prerequisite for promotion.

Not that ERGs haven't been popular with the people in them. Nearly every major company, for example, has introduced women's networks, run by women for women. Many participants love them; they enjoy talking together and sharing strategies for coping with male-dominated corporate cultures (often criticized by skeptical men as "wine and whine" sessions). As one woman in a prominent law firm told me, "It is the only place I feel I can be myself."

A lot of white men also liked this approach to managing diversity, because sponsoring or setting up an ERG offers a feel-good sensation of "doing something," but the reality was that few of these networks were properly funded, their leaders were usually doing all the work in their spare time, and the visibility they gained from running an ERG didn't necessarily serve them well in getting a promotion to a big operational role in the business.

Over the decades, these efforts too often became a convenient excuse for a lack of progress. Their continued presence today allows in-group men to say they "support women" (or people of color or LGBTQ employees) and then explain the lack of representation at the top as a lack of will or skill or ambition.

In the end, as Deloitte rightly points out, these networks divide people up into artificial subgroups (which group does a black lesbian join?) and isolate them from the networks of power and influence that are such a key part of how leaders identify and promote people.

As the American population and corporate talent pools grow ever more diverse, the meaning of "diversity" is shifting. The sum of all the groups considered to be minorities ends up being something entirely new: the majority. In this context, what was a radical idea in 1970 seems especially backward. Why tell the out-groups they have to figure out how to fit in, instead of teaching the in-groups how to reach out?

Women make up more than half of university graduates in many countries; earn the most masters and doctorate degrees in the United States today; and are becoming the majority of customers, end users, and regulators in an ever-expanding range of businesses.[2] They are the majority of many large companies' graduate intakes. Framing them as a special interest group has not been a useful way to address the business opportunities of an increasingly female talent pool and customer base.

Today's diversity challenge isn't getting more people to adapt to obsolete norms of leadership preferred by baby boomer white men. The challenge is to get all managers—and especially current leaders—skilled and ready to lead vastly more-diverse businesses and respond to increasingly diverse customer groups.

If ERGs framed inclusion as a special-interest-group issue, then Deloitte's shift to eliminate them is a powerful reframing. It's a way of saying that diversity is everyone's issue and that the dominant group is who needs to evolve.

Deb DeHaas, Deloitte's chief inclusion officer, sums it up clearly: "The key to unleashing the power of our diversity is inclusion. To us, inclusion is leadership in action. . . . It's everyone's responsibility, every day and at every level, to create the culture that can make that happen."[3]

The reality is that most female CEOs who get appointed to the top are selected, groomed, and appointed by male leaders. Xerox's Anne Mulcahy, IBM's Ginni Rometty, and GM's Mary Barra are the result of CEOs and companies that had pushed for better gender balance for decades. Google recently gender balanced its top team not because of incremental, organizational diversity efforts but because the CEO, Sundar Pichai, decided to appoint six women and seven men to run the business. Meanwhile, the rest of the tech sector continues to insist that such qualified women are impossible to find. Sad as I am to have to admit it, the future of female leadership in business is still in male hands.

Which leaves us with the task ahead: to educate and persuade today's dominant group that inclusion is good for business. We won't do that without making it their issue and responsibility. That's where Deloitte and some other global innovators are headed. The question now is, Who will follow?

————

Avivah Wittenberg-Cox is CEO of 20-First, one of the world's leading gender consulting firms, and the author of *Seven Steps to Leading a Gender-Balanced Business* (Harvard Business Review Press, 2014).

NOTES

1. Jeff Green, "Deloitte Thinks Diversity Groups Are Passé," *Bloomberg Businessweek*, July 24, 2017, 15–16.

2. Paula Bruggeman and Hillary Chan, "Minding the Gap: Tapping the Potential of Women to Transform Business," research report RR-16-01, Graduate Management Admission Council, March 28, 2016.

3. "DiversityInc Top 50, No. 12: Deloitte," Diversity Inc., 2017.

CHAPTER 27

Tackle Bias in Your Company Without Making People Defensive

by Avivah Wittenberg-Cox

Unconscious bias is all the rage. Every manager can learn from what's been written on this topic: the excellent book *The Invention of Difference* by Jo and Binna Kandola, the four-part "Women at Work" series by Sheryl Sandberg and Adam Grant in the *New York Times*, or the various articles by Herminia Ibarra, Robin Ely, Deborah Kolb, Joan C. Williams, and others that have appeared in

---

Adapted from content posted on hbr.org, March 10, 2015 (product #H01XFR)

Harvard Business Review. And at our firm, we're seeing a sudden surge in interest for sessions on unconscious bias to address gender imbalances. It's a promising shift from the exclusively women-focused initiatives that have dominated corporate balancing efforts for the past couple of decades.

I applaud this progress, and to maximize its impact, I'd like to suggest a productive way of bringing bias to the table—without losing half your guests. While hitting people over the head with accusations of bias may be a satisfaction for some, it is not well received by many.

The chief diversity officers who ask us for these programs love them, but managers generally don't. Defensiveness, contempt, and stonewalling are all on pretty immediate display. Is there a better, less abrasive way to achieve the same outcome? Can we build more-inclusive management styles that leverage current talent and serve today's heterogeneous customers without alienating the people we want to engage? Yes, and it starts with what we call it. Focusing people on positive outcomes is far more motivating than accusing them of misbehavior—whether conscious or unconscious. And it's simple enough to do. It begins with branding.

Recently, we were invited to help with the launch of a company's gender initiative. They were all set with presentations that highlighted the gender imbalance in their management teams and framed the loss of female talent as a serious problem that needed management's attention. This is usually the default framing (we call it the unconscious bias of the gender teams). The head of diversity was going to announce, at the annual company management conference, that she was launching a series of unconscious bias training sessions on gender for the several hundred managers in the room.

The only problem was, this was a guaranteed, set-up-to-fail mechanism. How enthusiastic do you think the people in the room—80% of them men—were going to be to hear that? Most of your company's managers, male or female, are probably committed to the idea that their company's systems are based on a meritocracy principle. They don't like being accused of gender bias before they even enter the room. The fact that all humans are biased to some degree is well researched. And addressing that reality is key. But there are more effective ways to bring the topic into companies. It starts with flipping the issue from a divisive, negative problem to a unifying, shared opportunity.

Begin by focusing on the key strategic goals. What are the five-year objectives, targets, and milestones you'd like to achieve? Get the CEO to start there. And then suggest that gender balance is a lever to help you reach those goals. Here's an example of this more positive framing from a real company we've worked with:

> We set a bold target of hitting $10 billion in revenue within the next five years. Getting the very best talent and delivering the very best customer service will be the dual keys to our success. Understanding, antici-pating, and delighting customers means ensuring we know what they want and how they feel. That requires having the best balance of talent in-house, talent that gets where our fast-changing market is heading. I

*believe gender balance is one of the key levers to unlock-
ing huge, untapped talent and market opportunities.
Today's talent pool is balanced—so are our customers.
We want to reflect that reality inside. So we are going
to focus on leadership skills and tools to build balanced
teams that continually deliver stellar service.*

This "tone from the top" has a different impact. It results, from the start, with a more engaged, less defensive
management team.

So, if you are working on launching or accelerating
a push for more gender balance in your company, ask
yourself some questions in these three areas:

- **Strategic opportunity:** Are you positioning gender
  as a problem or as an opportunity?

- **Positive branding:** Are you using language that
  accuses or language that invites the audience to
  build skills and enhance leadership impact?

- **Authentic leadership:** Are you engaging with the
  majority of your managers on things they understand are central to both their individual and
  company success? Or are your efforts perceived
  as politically correct, tick-the-box exercises?

It is an important moment on the road to more-
balanced businesses. But the final goal isn't balance. The
goal is more-engaged employees and more-connected
customers. You probably can't repeat that too often.
Leaders need to keep everyone's eye on that ball, while
drawing everyone into the game.

Best-in-class companies are moving on from an era of overfocusing on women as the solution to balance. Now they are focusing on managers. It's an unprecedented opportunity to get everyone positively primed for balance. Let's not lose them by accusing them. Companies are spending a lot of time and money on leadership. Let's make sure that whatever leadership model you work with, gender "bilingualism" is built in. We must practice what we preach about leading inclusively.

Avivah Wittenberg-Cox is CEO of 20-First, one of the world's leading gender consulting firms, and the author of *Seven Steps to Leading a Gender-Balanced Business* (Harvard Business Review Press, 2014).

CHAPTER 28

The Men Who Mentor Women

by Anna Marie Valerio and Katina Sawyer

Women make up 51.5% of all managers, and many fewer women than men rise to the C-suite.[1] A survey of 25,000 Harvard Business School graduates found that although male and female graduates had similar levels of ambition, men were significantly more likely to have positions in senior management, direct reports, and profit-and-loss responsibility.[2]

We know having a sponsor who supports your career can help level the playing field for women. So who are the men in your organization who are known as informal champions of women and for the way their behaviors

---

Adapted from content posted on hbr.org, December 7, 2016 (product #H03A54)

advance female leaders? And what do those men have in common?

From previous research, we already know that these "male champions" genuinely believe in fairness, gender equity, and the development of talent in their organizations—and that they are easily identified by female leaders for the critical role they play in advancing women's careers.

But we wanted to know more about what these men do differently. How do they stand up to pressure from peers or the expectations of outmoded organizational cultures? How do they use their power to create diverse, inclusive organizations?

We asked senior male and female leaders in *Fortune* 500 companies and nonprofit organizations to tell us about the behaviors of male champions. We conducted 75 semistructured confidential interviews with leaders in the C-suite or one to three levels below. After subjecting these interviews to a rigorous qualitative analysis, we saw several themes emerge.

Generally, we saw that male champions have learned that gender inclusiveness means involving *both* men and women in advancing women's leadership. As we learned in chapter 26, although many organizations have attempted to fight gender bias by focusing on women—offering training programs or networking groups specifically for them—the leaders we interviewed realized that any solutions that involve only 50% of the human population are likely to have limited success.

More specifically, we found that some of the key behavioral themes associated with gender inclusive leadership that support women's career advancement are:

- Using their authority to push workplace culture toward gender equality

- Thinking of gender inclusiveness as part of effective talent management

- Providing gender-aware mentoring and coaching

- Practicing other-focused leadership, not self-focused leadership

Using Authority to Change Workplace Culture

As researchers, we know that gender parity in the workplace is associated with improved profitability. Companies with female board representation have been found to outperform those with no women on their boards. Gender parity has been found to correlate with increased sales revenue, more customers, and greater relative profits. Companies in the top quartile for gender diversity were found to be 15% more likely to outperform those in the bottom quartile.[3]

In our experience, most executives don't know about this research. But even so, many of the leaders told us that gender inclusiveness is simply good strategy for the organization, and they explicitly used their authority to push for it.

For example, one leader addressed the business logic for diversity and inclusion, stating, "Let's do cost/benefit. If we are excluding half the talent on the planet . . . [do] we have the best chance of getting the best talent, or if we doubled our chances of getting the best talent do you think we'd have the best chance? Obviously, we want to fish in a bigger pond." Another leader emphasized that a lack of diversity demonstrates a lack of effectiveness in systems, noting, "My experience is when you get to very high levels, whether it's government, higher education, or business, there are excellent men and women. So if you're really not making good progress toward having representation at all levels of the company, you're doing something wrong."

Adopting this attitude has an impact on the overall culture of the organization. As one of our leaders described her male champion, "He's creating the environment that says, 'I care about all,' and that may be broader than just women, but it's modeling an environment that makes it harder for others not to be champions, too."

Another leader mentioned that he had built so much trust within his organization that he was able to single-handedly champion women into very high positions of power: "I can walk into the executive committee and say, 'This woman deserves to be on the bench two to three years from now. I want her to become the CEO.'" In a more nuanced way, another leader championed women by vying for them when they were in positions where success may have been unlikely, noting, "I was in a position of power to do something, and I suggested coaching for one woman whose direct boss was not very good. I just did the little things you do for someone to position them to move up in the organization."

While they were able to have a strong impact on women's careers in many ways, the male champions also recognized that their values were not always shared by others in their organizations. Leaders reported the need to show courage and persistence in order to overcome re-sistance to gender inclusiveness even in their own teams and peer groups.

One described the ways in which he pushes back on nondiverse pipelines directly: "I have what I call 'talent days,' in which my management team spends the whole day once a quarter, and we look through our organization for rising stars and identify people early. The other thing that we do is we try to make sure we have proactive inter-viewing. For any position, we have leading and lagging metrics for diversity. And I ask them: 'How come, in the last month, you've gone after a large number of new peo-ple, and you haven't interviewed one woman for the posi-tion?' I started asking questions like this—I am not ex-pecting them to have the answers. I'm expecting them to know that the next time I ask these questions, you better have the answers because I already have the data."

Similarly, one of our champions mentioned the im-portance of pushing back on gender stereotypes, saying, "I think just having the courage to raise the questions is important. If I'm in a people review with all the busi-ness leads, and we're talking about behaviors and we're saying, this woman is just really aggressive—the Scar-let A!—then I ask them, 'Are we talking about it with al-most the exact same behaviors as a male, in a very com-plementary way?' So being able to have the courage to raise those questions, and not in an antagonistic fashion but more in a very constructive, nonjudgmental way, is very important."

Finally, one the females who had been championed, summed up the role these men play in her company, saying, "Many of these men with whom I worked clearly were very comfortable in their own skin and believed in the values of having equity in the workplace and were willing to stand up and fight for it."

Recognizing Inclusiveness as Effective Talent Management

Although many of the male leaders said they had not known they were considered to be male champions until recommended for the research study, examples of their behavior show that they practiced talent management that was effective for gender inclusion, using best-practice strategies in recruitment, early identification of talent, and succession planning. For example, a leader described his hiring process, detailing, "We'll remember if we hired the absolute best person for the job, which includes considering women and building diversity in our team. So I hold the jobs open, and we've never lowered the bar. That's probably not that unique, but I make sure we have a slate of candidates that includes all who are qualified for the job."

Similarly, another leader noted, "It's not particularly hard for me to make sure that we have a slate of candidates that are qualified folks that include women." Other leaders mentioned that they were consciously consistent about ensuring that men and women were given the same opportunities on their teams. For example, one leader stated, "We do have mentor programs, we do have emergent leader programs, and we have [other programs] that require executives and senior VP-types within the business to participate. It makes the high potentials better leaders." Another leader noted, "I always try to get at least 50% women in my groups, and I've been pretty successful at doing that. My current group I think is 80% women, and there's a lot of research that shows you need diversity, and it's just smart to do that."

Providing Gender-Aware Mentoring and Coaching

Mentoring was recently found to be the most impactful activity for increasing diversity and inclusion at work, compared with diversity training and a variety of other diversity initiatives.[4] Receiving mentorship from senior males can increase compensation and career progress satisfaction for women, particularly for those working in male-dominated industries.

Many champions made special efforts to provide visibility to talented women through mentoring and coaching. For example, a leader mentioned strategically exposing women to the leadership process, stating, "One of the things I would often do is take one of our high-performing women executives and make them chief of staff to me so they would run my office, participate in executive committee meetings, format the meetings, really be an extension of my office to give them an opportunity to see the world top down and to work with other senior executives, which was a very important developmental experience for them."

Other leaders mentioned that they helped coach women by providing necessary skills that they would need to get the job done. For example, one leader recounted a conversation with a female he championed, stating, "She said, 'I'm not sure if I'm good enough to do the job.' I said, 'Well, I think you really are so let's talk about where you feel you need more development.' So if they're not confident before they have the job, you've got to be proactive and ask them, 'What do you need to be comfortable with that job?'"

One of our champions mentioned that understanding the goals of the women he has championed was also important, saying, "They don't necessarily have the visibility either because of the roles they're in or because they're not necessarily getting sponsored. . . . We expand their visibility but also arm them with experiences that will broaden their perspective and therefore enable them to compete even more effectively for big roles."

Women leaders also recognize when opportunities for visibility are provided to them. One of our female interviewees mentioned, "I realized before I gave the presentation, thankfully, that he was giving me a huge opportunity to be seen by a much broader audience, and he never made a lot fanfare about it. He never told me that he wanted to help my career. He just did." Similarly, another female interviewee highlighted the importance of being let into strategic networks, stating, "I often went to lunch with him when he went to lunch with people. I sat in on a lot of phone calls." In the same vein, another female interviewee mentioned that being privy to new people within the organization was helpful in career advancement, noting, "You get increased contacts across the organization and more senior contacts than you typically would, because even if you haven't met somebody, if they've seen your name on a report or heard of your name with regard to a high-profile project, when you do meet them, they already know who you are."

As a result of the mentoring and coaching, many women reported feeling greater self-confidence, which gave them the comfort of doing even more. One female interviewee stated, "The outcome of some of these actions that my male mentors took is that they helped me understand I had a lot more capacity than even I knew." Similarly, another female interviewee mentioned, "It's building self-confidence. It gives you the confidence that you belong at the table and that you have a right to be there."

Practicing Other-Focused Leadership

For cross-gender mentoring relationships to be successful, Simmons College professor Stacy D. Blake-Beard suggests that mentors need to possess both crucial mentoring skills and an ally mentality. Allies are "dominant group members who work to end prejudice in their personal and professional lives and relinquish social privileges conferred by their group status through their support of nondominant groups" in the commonly used definition.[5]

Enabling the development of others' leadership requires moving away from a focus on one's personal power so that others may be recognized for their achievements. Many of the male champions we interviewed embodied this spirit of leadership as an exercise for others—not for oneself.

One leader explained, "How many people can you point to who are in leadership positions in the company because they worked for you and with you, and you helped make them better? A lot of times people want to hire what I call 'younger brothers and sisters' that are not threatening and not really as effective as they need to be. Your job is to hire and develop people who can be better than you, if they're not better than you to begin with."

A female interviewee concurred, stating, "I also think that there might be some level of altruism too, right? They're doing it for the greater good of the organization and not necessarily having a strategic goal in mind. But it's the right thing to be doing for people."

Through behaviors like these, men can begin to change organizational cultures from the top down. Acknowledging the crucial role that men can play in creating gender equality is necessary to truly engage the entire workforce in conversations surrounding equality and fairness at work. The examples provided by male champions and female leaders who have been championed by them contain important leadership lessons, useful for any organization interested in promoting gender inclusivity at work.

————————

Anna Marie Valerio, PhD, is an executive coach and the author of two books, *Developing Women Leaders: A Guide for Men and Women in Organizations* and *Executive Coaching: A Guide for the HR Professional* (co-authored with Robert J. Lee). She is president of Executive Leadership Strategies, LLC. **Katina Sawyer, PhD,** is an assistant professor of management in the School of Business at the George Washington University. She was formerly an assistant professor of psychology in the graduate program in human resource development at Villanova University. She holds a dual PhD in industrial/ organizational psychology and women's studies from the Pennsylvania State University.

NOTES

1. U.S. Department of Labor, Bureau of Labor Statistics, "Employed Persons by Detailed Occupation, Sex, Race, and Hispanic or Latino Ethnicity," 2017, https://www.bls.gov/cps/cpsaat11.pdf.

2. Robin J. Ely, Pamela Stone, and Colleen Ammerman, "Rethink What You 'Know' About High-Achieving Women," *Harvard Business Review*, December 2014 (product #R1412G).

3. Vivian Hunt, Dennis Layton, and Sara Prince, "Why Diversity Matters," McKinsey & Company, January 2015, https://www.mckinsey.com/business-functions/organization/our-insights/why-diversity-matters.

4. Frank Dobbin and Alexandra Kalev, "Why Diversity Programs Fail," *Harvard Business Review*, July–August 2016 (product #R1607C).

5. Kendrick T. Brown and Joan M. Ostrove, "What Does It Mean to Be an Ally? The Perception of Allies from the Perspective of People of Color," *Journal of Applied Psychology* 43, no. 11 (October 18, 2013): 2211–2222.

CHAPTER 29

Stop "Protecting" Women from Challenging Work

by Kristen Jones and Eden King

A 2016 poll by the Pew Research Center suggests that more than half of men think sexism is a thing of the past. In contrast, only about one-third of women agree. One reason for the disagreement may stem from misunderstandings about the kinds of behavior that constitute sexism. Indeed, an important body of research conducted by Susan Fiske of Princeton and Peter Glick of Lawrence University demonstrates that prejudice toward women can take obvious and not-so-obvious

---

Adapted from content posted on hbr.org, September 9, 2016 (product #H034DE)

forms.[1] Both forms are destructive. But our research shows that this latter "benevolent" form of sexism is exceptionally damaging, particularly in the workplace. It primarily manifests itself in two ways.

First, much like the way anxious new parents shield their children from potentially harmful situations, managers often see women as being in need of protection, so they limit their exposure to risky or challenging work. For example, surveys of men and women in the oil and gas and health care industries show that women received fewer challenging developmental work opportunities than men.[2] Both men and women, however, reported comparable levels of interest in engaging in these assignments. Follow-up experiments confirmed that managers who engage in benevolent sexism "protected" women from challenging assignments and instead gave the work to men. While this may have seemed nice on the surface, these behaviors actually made it more difficult for women to advance.

Second, women are less likely to get constructive criticism and more likely to receive unsolicited offers for help. But although well-intentioned, such attempts to protect or coddle women can undermine their self-confidence. In the earlier-mentioned survey, supervisors gave female managers less negative feedback than their male counterparts. But constructive criticism has been found to be essential for increased performance and learning. (For tips on how to give fair feedback, see the sidebar "Improving Feedback for Women.")

In another experiment, fake teammates told some undergraduate participants who were working on a task,

IMPROVING FEEDBACK FOR WOMEN

by Shelley Correll and Caroline Simard

Managers can improve the feedback they give and start leveling the playing field at the team level with a few simple steps:

- Before you begin evaluations, either written or verbal, outline the specific criteria you are employing to evaluate individuals. Articulate the specific results or behaviors that would demonstrate mastery. Use the same criteria for all employees at this level.

- Set a goal to discuss three specific business outcomes with all employees. If you can't think of those outcomes for a particular employee, dig deeper or ask the employee or their peers to provide more details.

- Systematically tie feedback—either positive or developmental—to business and goals outcomes. If you find yourself giving feedback without relating it to outcomes (such as, "People like working with you"), ask yourself whether you can further tie the feedback to specific results (such as, "You are effective at building team outcomes. You successfully resolved the divide between the engineering team and the product

(continued)

IMPROVING FEEDBACK FOR WOMEN

(*continued*)

team on which features to prioritize in our last sprint, leading us to ship the product on time").

- When evaluating people in similar roles, equalize references to technical accomplishments and capability. Notice when detail is lacking for a particular employee, and make an extra effort to determine whether something, either a skill or a developmental need, has been missed.

- Strive to write reviews of similar lengths for all employees. This helps ensure a similar level of detail—and therefore of specifics—for everyone.

These small wins, or what we call micro-sponsorship actions, offer pathways to equal access to leadership.

———

Shelley Correll is a professor of sociology and organizational behavior at Stanford University, the Barbara D. Finberg Director of the Clayman Institute for Gender Research, and the Faculty Director of the Center for the Advancement of Women's Leadership. **Caroline Simard** is senior research director at the Center for the Advancement of Women's Leadership at Stanford University.

Adapted from "Research: Vague Feedback Is Holding Women Back" on hbr.org, April 29, 2016 (product #H02UUL)

"Let me help you with this. I know this kind of thing can be hard for some girls/guys."[3] Both male and female participants who were treated in this "benevolent" manner felt worse about their own ability than participants who were not helped. A separate survey of working adults reported in the same paper confirmed these findings. This type of patronizing yet seemingly positive behavior undermines self-efficacy: It is assumptive (rather than requested), it implies that its recipient is dependent on (rather than autonomous from) the provider of support, and it is asserted didactically (rather than negotiated through discussion). Importantly, women are more likely to be the recipients of this type of unwanted help and therefore are more likely to suffer its negative consequences.

Yet many of these problems have clear solutions. Attempts to support women at work may be most effective when they occur in response to a request, when they enable rather than restrict autonomy, and when they are negotiated through discussion. For example, rather than assuming that a woman would say no to an assignment involving travel, just *ask* her. Instead of telling a woman she should take an extended maternity leave, inquire as to how long she would *like* to take. When attempting to support female employees, managers should think carefully about how and why they are motivated to do so, whether they would support a male employee in the same manner, and what implicit message their behavior is sending to the woman.

Does this mean chivalry is dead? No. All people like to be treated with courtesy and respect. But it does mean that some behaviors—those that are patronizing, overly protective, and unsolicited—can be harmful. Women can get by with a little less of this kind of help from their colleagues.

Kristen Jones is an assistant professor of management in the Fogelman College of Business and Economics at the University of Memphis. Her research focuses on identifying and remediating subtle bias that unfairly disadvantages diverse employees at work, particularly women and mothers. **Eden King** is an associate professor of Psychology at Rice University and an associate editor of the *Journal of Management* and the *Journal of Business and Psychology*. She has published more than 100 scholarly works related to discrimination, including the book *How Women Can Make It Work: The Science of Success*.

NOTES

1. Peter Glick and Susan T. Fiske, "An Ambivalent Alliance: Hostile and Benevolent Sexism as Complementary Justifications for Gender Inequality," *American Psychologist* 56, no. 2 (February 2001): 109–118.

2. Eden B. King et al., "Benevolent Sexism at Work: Gender Differences in the Distribution of Challenging Developmental Experiences," *Journal of Management* 38, no. 6 (November 1, 2012): 1835–1866.

3. Kristen Jones, et al., "Negative Consequences of Benevolent Sexism on Efficacy and Performance," *Gender in Management: An International Journal* 29, no. 3 (2014): 171–189.

Index

Smart advice and inspiration from a source you trust.

If you enjoyed this book and want more comprehensive guidance on essential professional skills, turn to the HBR Guides Boxed Set. Packed with the practical advice you need to succeed, this seven-volume collection provides smart answers to your most pressing work challenges, from writing more effective emails and delivering persuasive presentations to setting priorities and managing up and across.

Harvard Business Review Guides

Available in paperback or ebook format. Plus, find downloadable tools and templates to help you get started.

- Better Business Writing
- Building Your Business Case
- Buying a Small Business
- Coaching Employees
- Delivering Effective Feedback
- Finance Basics for Managers
- Getting the Mentoring You Need
- Getting the Right Work Done

- Leading Teams
- Making Every Meeting Matter
- Managing Stress at Work
- Managing Up and Across
- Negotiating
- Office Politics
- Persuasive Presentations
- Project Management

HBR.ORG/GUIDES

Buy for your team, clients, or event.
Visit hbr.org/bulksales for quantity discount rates.

Harvard Business Review Press

The most important management ideas all in one place.

We hope you enjoyed this book from *Harvard Business Review*. For the best ideas HBR has to offer turn to HBR's 10 Must Reads Boxed Set. From books on leadership and strategy to managing yourself and others, this 6-book collection delivers articles on the most essential business topics to help you succeed.

HBR's 10 Must Reads Series

The definitive collection of ideas and best practices on our most sought-after topics from the best minds in business.

- Change Management
- Collaboration
- Communication
- Emotional Intelligence
- Innovation
- Leadership
- Making Smart Decisions
- Managing Across Cultures
- Managing People
- Managing Yourself
- Strategic Marketing
- Strategy
- Teams
- The Essentials

hbr.org/mustreads

Notes

Notes

Notes

Notes

Notes